CANNABIS 101

By Dan Ulloa

1st Edition

From Heady NJ

Headynj.com

Cannabis 101

ISBN 9781393562726

dan@headynj.com

(908) 421-1422

Table of Contents

Author's Note

This book is intended for those who want to learn about cannabis and those who are always interested in learning more about the nuances of its history, politics, legal status, and the industry that has sprung forth around it. While this book seeks to be reasonably comprehensive, I do not consider myself to be an expert in every aspect of cannabis. Other, better-known writers have covered cannabis agriculture, horticulture, and science.

CHAPTER 1

CANNABIS THROUGHOUT HISTORY

C annabis has been harvested since the beginning of time. The plant has been developed from its raw form for industrial, medical, and recreational purposes. Flower from the plant is dried, crushed, and smoked to get high. "High" is both the colloquial and technical term to describe what happens when an individual consumes the plant, typically by smoking. Its stalks produce a wide variety of industrial products. The industrial form of cannabis is known as hemp. The federal government uses the term "marijuana" to refer to cannabis that gets you high, and "hemp" to refer to cannabis used for industrial purposes that cannot get you high. Hemp is like marijuana the way Poodles and Dobermans are both dogs.

The cultivation of cannabis originated in ancient Taiwan and China.[1] From there, it went to India and then slowly spread across the planet. (There's a reason it's called weed.) Ancient civilizations, including the Ancient Greeks and others, used it. Proponents maintain that specific Bible passages refer to cannabis. For example, scholars have argued that cannabis was one of the ingredients God instructed Moses to use when creating Holy Oil for the priests of the Israelites to use during rituals.[2]

Over time, the use of cannabis to make industrial products such as rope and paper became well known. During the Renaissance and afterward, the powerful Republic of Venice began the use of hemp for rope, sails, and linen to maintain their navy.[3] In 2019, South African scientists analyzed fragments of a pipe on the grounds of William Shakespeare's home and found that it contained particles of cannabis.[4]

Hemp was a cash crop in Colonial America. It was in such high demand that Colonial Virginia required farmers to grow hemp.[5] For this reason, George Washington and Thomas Jefferson grew hemp.[6] Jefferson used hemp paper to write early drafts of the Declaration of Independence. It is not known whether the Founding Fathers got high or not.[7]

However, we do know that George Washington wrote that he "sowed hemp [presumably Indian hemp] at muddy hole by swamp" (May 12-13, 1765); this indicates he was growing it away from the hemp he grew for fiber. "Began to separate the male from female plants at do [sic]—rather too late" (August 7, 1765), and, "Pulling up the (male)hemp. Was too late for the blossom hemp by three weeks or a month" (August 29, 1766).[8] This indicates that he was trying to grow female plants, which are grown for smoking.[9]

During the 19th century, cannabis was commonly used as medicine in the United States and Western Europe. Queen Victoria's doctor prescribed it to her to treat migraines from menstruation.[10] The *U.S. Pharmacopoeia*, the foremost authority on medicine, listed it as an official type of medicine in its editions published from 1851 to 1942.

A bottle of medical marijuana from the 19ᵗʰ century

In the 19ᵗʰ century, hashish or hash became popular in the United States and Europe for recreational use. Hashish is made by pressing cannabis into a small square that is usually consumed by smoking. It was also called "Indian Hemp" in the United States since it thrived in India during the era of the British Raj. The cannabis given to Queen Victoria was from India.

The 1906 Pure Food and Drug Act required cannabis to be labeled on medicine bottles, and it slowly fell out of use. The problem was that many began to think it was as harmful as cocaine or heroin. Before the passage of the 1906 Act, drugs were largely unregulated in the United

States. This led to the recognition that "snake oil," which included a variety of chemicals in a bottle sold as medicine that could be harmful.

According to an article by William Breathes, more Mexicans began immigrating to the United States in the 1910s and were enthusiastic users of cannabis (called marijuana in Spanish) for recreational purposes.[11] They began the custom of passing around a joint. It is unlikely they were using the Indian hemp brought from India. Rather they likely used a version derived from hemp the Spanish brought to the Americas in the 16th century for industrial purposes.[12] Mexican American immigrants brought it to New Orleans, a center of jazz music.[13] Many famous jazz musicians subsequently became cannabis enthusiasts.

Cannabis was included when the cry came from prohibitionists to regulate opium. Moreover, Mexican immigrants faced a backlash against their arrival in the United States, which made many oppose them and decry their "marijuana." The cry for prohibition became louder, and states started making cannabis illegal in the 1910s.

In 1930 Harry Anslinger was appointed the first commissioner of the Federal Bureau of Narcotics (FBN) during the Hoover administration. Initially, his job was to stamp out illegal heroin and cocaine. But this was a minor problem at the time. After alcohol became legal again in 1933, it seemed his already small bureau would shrink even further. So Anslinger seized on anti-cannabis sentiment and fanned the flames.[14] He developed a campaign for the prohibition of cannabis that became widespread.

The effort was led in the media by William Randolph Hearst. His national newspaper chain ran stories decrying the ills of cannabis where a crime had been committed (usually by a minority), and cannabis seemed to be involved. Most were either false or obscured the real reason the crime was committed (mental illness independent of cannabis use, for example).[15] Hearst owned large timber companies and may have seen hemp as a threat to his interests.[16] Others say he ran the stories because he was racist. Many say the company DuPont was in favor of cannabis prohibition because if hemp could be outlawed, then their synthetically derived products would have less competition. Those who believe in this theory say U.S. Treasury Secretary Andrew Mellon, who appointed Anslinger, wanted cannabis to become illegal because his bank would profit since DuPont was a major client. Hemp production has been in decline though since the Civil War since it was economically prohibitive to refine it in contrast to other fibers. The technology was being developed at the time that would have brought industrialization to hemp and made it easier to process.[17]

The film *Reefer Madness* was released in 1936. In the movie, seemingly wholesome teenagers degenerate when a gangster gives them weed. Seen now, it comes across as exaggerated and comical. While it was not commercially successful, the values it espoused became widespread.

The prohibitionist campaign smeared cannabis as something that African American musicians and Mexican American immigrants used; they preferred the term "marihuana" to associate with the foreign Mexicans. Thus, the drug "marijuana" was made illegal in the 1937 Marihuana Tax Stamp Act. No one used the term marijuana before the prohibitionist campaign. It is not clear why the federal government chose the spelling "Marihuana" and not "Marijuana." Because marijuana has such a racially charged history, the preferred nomenclature is cannabis.

The marijuana prohibitionist campaign faced almost no organized opposition. The only group that fought them was the American Medical Association because of its history for medical uses. Ironically, they are now against all uses of cannabis. Many did not know the difference between the medicinal version and the type being smoked recreationally. Two people were quickly arrested after the passage of the law to make an example. They were not even aware that cannabis prohibition had been passed.

Mayor Fiorello LaGuardia of New York City was not convinced that cannabis should be illegal. Therefore, he commissioned the New York Association of Medicine to study the issue. They produced what's known as the "LaGuardia Report," which found that "The practice of smoking marihuana does not lead to addiction in the medical sense of the word ... The use of marihuana does not lead to morphine or heroin or cocaine addiction and no effort is made to create a market for these narcotics by stimulating the practice of marihuana smoking... Marihuana is not the determining factor in the commission of major crimes... The publicity concerning the catastrophic effects of marihuana smoking in New York City is unfounded."[18]

Hemp is so effective as a material to make rope that during World War II, the federal government temporarily allowed farmers to grow it and encouraged its production. To do so, they commissioned the film "Hemp for Victory," which illustrated its many uses and told farmers it was their patriotic duty to grow hemp.[19]

Even though it is was made illegal, people secretly continued enjoying the effects of cannabis. Louis Armstrong consumed cannabis throughout his career. His dealer was a jazz musician named Milton "Mezz" Mezzrow, who became so famous for dealing that his nickname was shorthand for a joint in the '40s. Mezzrow sold cannabis in Harlem and Chicago. If an authority figure were around, one could ask for a Mezz without fear of being caught. Along with Armstrong, major jazz and big band musicians loved cannabis, including Tommy Dorsey, Benny Goodman, Cab Calloway, Billie Holiday, Nat King Cole, and Ella Fitzgerald. They all recorded songs explicitly describing the enjoyment of cannabis.[20]

Others continued getting high as well. In the 1950s, Jack Kerouac wrote about using it in his well-known book *On the Road*.[21] In the

1960s, it became ingrained within the counterculture that rose among the youth. Around this time, a few high school students in Northern California began to meet after school at 4:20 pm to smoke.[22] Calling it "420" was a convenient way to discuss cannabis in front of figures who would not support their use. They later became followers of the Grateful Dead with whom they had personal connections. 420's connection to cannabis was subsequently spread through hippie culture and the underground cannabis culture through their followers, the Deadheads. Thus, due to the time 4:20, the date April 20th became a day to celebrate cannabis use.

Also, in the 1960s, Rastafarianism from Jamaica came to the United States through reggae music. Rastafarianism is a religion that's an offshoot of Christianity in which smoking cannabis is considered a spiritual practice, akin to drinking wine in Christianity and Judaism. Rastafarians call cannabis "Ganja" and use it as a sacrament in their spiritual practices. Ganja arrived in the Caribbean from Indian laborers in the 19th century.

Rastafarians believe that Haile Selassie, the late Emperor of Ethiopia, is the true messiah. Before being proclaimed Emperor, his name was Ras Tafari, which became the name of the new religion. The fact that he was the only ruler of a free black country in Africa was appealing to the Jamaicans who adopted this new belief system. Even his death in 1975 did not deter the Rastafarians from believing he was the messiah.

Rastafarianism includes earlier civil rights beliefs. It also seeks to empower the economically oppressed. They refer to the West, where Blacks are treated as second class citizens, as "Babylon." Many Rastafarians seek to return to Africa, which they call "Zion."[23]

Numerous reggae musicians from Jamaica believed in this religion. Bob Marley and the Wailers, who were adherents, became the most famous reggae band and toured the United States. The other two members of the band were Peter Tosh and Bunny Wailer. Marley later broke from them and toured as a solo act. Marley emphasized Rastafarian principles in his songs and wore dreadlocks in the Rastafarian custom. Thus, the Jamaican colors of Gold, Red, and Green, and images of Marley are found throughout weed culture.

A stylized image of Bob Marley with Rastafarian colors of green, yellow, and red left to right

In the 1970s, the Netherlands decided to liberalize its drug policy. They created a market where it's legal for coffeehouses to sell five grams of cannabis along with cannabis oil, including their famous pot brownies.[24] But it's illegal for the coffeeshops to purchase in bulk quantity. So, a strange market exists whereby coffeehouses buy cannabis illegally and then sell it legally. Wholesaling remains technically illegal.

Other restrictions in the Netherlands include the prohibition of explicit advertising, selling more than 500 grams to one customer, selling to children, selling within 250 meters of a school, selling cocaine, heroin, and LSD, and creating a "nuisance." Because of this, establishments that sell cannabis are known as "coffeeshops" rather than something like "cannabis lounges." They also are not allowed to sell alcohol or allow customers to consume tobacco.

The legal status of cannabis is a gray area. Small scale operations are overlooked because a significant percentage of the tourists who visit the Netherlands do so for the coffeehouses. While some towns in the Netherlands have an outright ban, Amsterdam remains a mecca for those seeking to visit the coffeeshops. Pressure from the rest of the European Union has since stopped the Netherlands from making cannabis fully legal.

In the late 1960s, noted drug activist and Harvard professor Timothy Leary was arrested for cannabis possession after purchasing grass in Mexico and crossing the border. He contested the case up to the Supreme Court. In 1969, the United States Supreme Court, in *Leary v. United States* (1969), sided with him and struck down the Marihuana Tax Act. The Supreme Court said that it violated the Fifth Amendment right against self-incrimination.[25] Thus cannabis briefly became legal again on the federal level. It was largely still illegal on the state level, though.

However, the 1970 Controlled Substances Act (CSA) made cannabis possession and distribution a more serious crime. President Richard Nixon advocated for enforcement to include arresting hippies and leftist radicals for possession to hamper their movements. It was verified that this was his intention by his former senior domestic policy advisor John Ehrlichman when he said,

"The Nixon campaign in 1968, and the Nixon White House after that, had two enemies: the antiwar left and black people. You understand what I'm saying? We knew we couldn't make it illegal to be either against the war or black, but by getting the public to associate the hippies with marijuana and blacks with heroin, and then criminalizing both heavily, we could disrupt those communities. We could arrest their leaders, raid their homes, break up their meetings, and vilify them night after night on the evening news. Did we know we were lying about the drugs? Of course we did."[26]

A commission to study the nature of cannabis was created as part of the CSA. Nixon appointed former Governor of Pennsylvania Raymond Shafer as its Chairman. The commission issued a report which said that cannabis was not harmful and should not be illegal.[27] The Nixon Administration ignored the report and sustained the War on Drugs. But Nixon's decision to clamp down on drugs did not achieve the outcome he sought. It certainly did not destroy the anti-war movement.

The establishment of the National Organization for Reform of Marijuana Laws (NORML) by Keith Stroup and others, with financial help from Hugh Hefner in the 1970s, led to a wave of decriminalization of cannabis on the state level across the country.[28] Current NORML Executive Director Erik Altieri said that Stroup worked with the Carter Administration, Dr. Lester Grinspoon, Willie Nelson, and noted astronomer Carl Sagan to push decriminalization. That led to the establishment of a cottage industry of cannabis paraphernalia sold in "head" shops and convenience stores. In 1974, Tom Forcade founded the magazine *High Times,* which was the premier cannabis publication in the country for many years. During his administration, former President Jimmy Carter called on Congress to decriminalize cannabis federally![29]

But a backlash occurred that coincided with the rise of the conservative movement.[30] Many parents thought that cannabis merchandise appealed to teenagers. They were outraged. Ronald Reagan led this movement against the liberalization of society and rode it into the White House in 1980. While President, he was a great proponent of the War on Drugs and escalated it by creating harsher penalties and arresting far more people. The number of people in prison for cannabis crimes rose from 50,000 in 1980 to 400,000 in 1997.[31]

(It is strange to have a war on a general term, like the War on

Terrorism. The nature of the name suggests because it is not on something specific; it can go on indefinitely.)

Concurrent with the escalation, First Lady Nancy's Reagan's "Just Say No" campaign became popular. The United States, under Reagan, sought to force other countries around the world to maintain a similar policy, including India, where respected holy men called "Sadhus" consume cannabis. Around the same time, a book by legendary activist Jack Herer called "The Emperor Wears No Clothes" was published; it detailed the history and benefits of cannabis/hemp and advocated for its legalization.

In the 1980s, when AIDs became an epidemic, certain caregivers and patients began realizing that cannabis could help them manage the negative side effects of the disease and its treatments. It began under the leadership of Dennis Peron, a San Francisco leader of a group seeking to bring relief to AIDS patients. Peron worked with a woman nicknamed "Brownie Mary," who became well-known for distributing weed brownies to AIDS patients free of charge in San Francisco.[32]

Thus, a movement began building in California to legalize cannabis for medical use through a ballot initiative. The passage of a referendum in 1996 legalized medical marijuana in California. Around that time, new organizations were formed in part to promote cannabis reform, including the Marijuana Policy Project (MPP); this group was founded by former NORML staffers who wanted to focus solely on lobbying.[33] The Drug Policy Alliance (DPA) was formed in 2000 when the Drug Policy Foundation and the Lindesmith Center merged.[34] Slowly, other states started following California in legalizing medical marijuana.

Colorado and Washington became the first states to make history by fully legalizing adult-use cannabis in 2012 though the passage of ballot initiatives. Before 2012, voters in Colorado, Washington, and California had defeated the approval of adult-use of cannabis.

In Colorado, it was not clear that the adult-use referendum would pass. While major cities such as Denver and Boulder are progressive, the residents of Colorado Springs and many rural areas are more conservative. However, Colorado's Amendment 64 ultimately passed by a comfortable 55 percent of the vote in 2012.[35]

The *Denver Post* opposed the measure, arguing that drug policy did not belong in the state constitution while claiming to support legalization in general. But the initiative received support from conservative sources, including former Congressman Tom Tancredo, a Republican who represented the state's Sixth Congressional district. He sent a letter to Republican state lawmakers saying, "Eighty years ago, Colorado voters concerned about the health and safety of their families and communities approved a ballot initiative to repeal alcohol prohibition prior to it being done by the federal government. This November, we have the opportunity to end the equally problematic and ineffective policy of marijuana prohibition."[36]

The initiative also received support from groups like the MPP and the American Civil Liberties Union (ACLU) that fight for legalization across the country.[37] Also, the state Green Party, the Libertarian Party of Colorado, its 2012 presidential candidate Gary Johnson, and the Colorado Criminal Defense Bar Association endorsed it.[38] The Campaign to Regulate Marijuana Like Alcohol ended up outraising the opposition with $3.7 million. Former Congressman and incumbent Colorado Governor Jared Polis (as of 2020) was a supporter of legalization while then-Governor John Hickenlooper was not (Both are Democrats).

"Today, the people of Colorado have rejected the failed policy of marijuana prohibition," said Brian Vicente, co-director of the Campaign to Regulate Marijuana when the measure passed. "Thanks to their votes, we will now reap the benefits of regulation. We will create new jobs, generation million (sic) of dollars in tax revenue and allow law enforcement to focus on serious crimes."[39]

In Washington, legalization came with a 25 percent sales tax, which made it attractive to those seeking a new source of tax revenue. The legalization campaign received broad support from NORML, the Drug Policy Alliance, the NAACP, the ACLU, the Law Enforcement Action Partnership (LEAP), the Mayor and City Council of Seattle, and the Sheriff of Kings County, which contains Seattle.[40] The referendum had the support of the State Democratic Party as well.[41] It also received support from *The Stranger*, a popular alternative newspaper in Seattle, *The Seattle Times*, other newspapers in the state, and from noted televangelist Pat Robertson.[42] While some law enforcement and parent groups opposed it, Initiative 502, as it was known, passed with 55 percent of the vote.

And so, the movement for adult-use cannabis spread across the country. Advocates joined on from different walks of life and experience to push legalization. Thus, 34 states have legalized medical cannabis, and 11 of those states and Washington, DC have legalized both adult-use and medical cannabis. West Virginia is the most recent state to have legalized medical marijuana, and thus their program has not yet begun to operate.

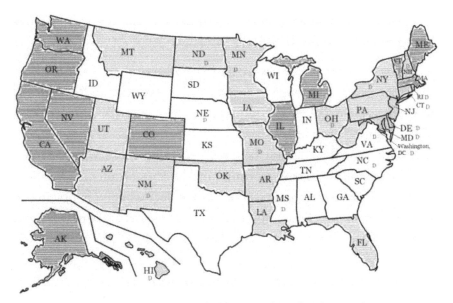

The dark states have legalized adult-use and medical cannabis. The light gray states have only legalized medical cannabis, and the white states have not approved either. A "D" indicates states where cannabis was decriminalized.

It cannot be emphasized enough how much the fight for the legalization of both medical and recreational cannabis has been fought thus far on the state level. This is why every state has different cannabis laws. Vermont and Washington, DC, have unique situations whereby while cannabis possession is legal, cannabis sales are not. Thus, a gray market has developed, especially in Washington. For example, at the History of Cannabis Museum in Washington, DC, the premium entrance fee includes a joint.[43] Other businesses require the purchase of a membership or a t-shirt for three times its normal amount and say cannabis then comes free with it!

Despite being officially illegal there, New York City is acknowledged as the city where consumption is the highest. An advanced system of home delivery has been operating for a while despite its status. Its illicit market is substantial.

Since the 1990s, more and more people have supported legalization; its support has since reached around 63 percent, making it one of the most popular issues in the country.[44] Support has been rising for cannabis among Democrats, Independents, and Republicans. It is now above 50 percent for all three groups, with support being highest among Democrats.

With cannabis' natural benefits becoming more widely known across the world, usage is growing quickly. Even women and seniors, once hesitant to engage in cannabis, are increasingly embracing its health benefits. Those 50 and older are the fastest-growing demographic of cannabis users because as it becomes legal and normalized, they are finding it an excellent solution to cope with the chronic pain and other ailments that come with aging.

However, before it becomes legal, it is still illegal, and there are consequences to possession and distribution charges. So be careful! Cops are still eager to catch those consuming in public, even in seemingly liberal areas. That is the case in some states close to legalization.

CHAPTER 2

THE NUANCES OF THE CANNABIS PLANT

The cannabis plant with its distinct leaves, flower, and trichomes
The scientific study of cannabis is fascinating. Cannabis plants are gendered, meaning there are both male and female plants. The cannabis that people smoke is grown from female plants. Trichomes are tiny white crystals on the plant that glisten in the light. The cannabinoids, flavonoids, and terpenes that make cannabis unique are contained in

the trichomes.[45] Trichomes protect the plant from insects and other elements found in nature. It is also what makes cannabis sticky.

Terpenes give cannabis its distinctive smell and produce some of its health benefits. There are more than 200 distinct terpenes in the cannabis plant. Flavonoids also contribute to the aroma of cannabis and its effectiveness as a medicine.[46] They bring out the color in the plant as it grows.

Cannabinoids are chemical compounds found in the plant. More than 113 cannabinoids have been discovered and classified thus far. Phytocannabinoids are produced in the trichomes of the cannabis plant.[47] The human body produces endocannabinoids. Both phytocannabinoids and endocannabinoids interact with the Endocannabinoid System (ECS).[48]

The ECS is a system of cannabinoid receptors in the human brain, the central nervous system, peripheral nervous system, and the immune system. Experts believe the ECS controls many functions in the body, including memory, mood regulation, stress management, cognitive performance, and pain perception, among others. It helps the body achieve homeostasis, a balance of compounds that is necessary for the body to function at its best. Many believe this is why cannabis is effective in medical treatment. It also points to the long history cannabis has of interacting with the human body.

The most significant of the cannabinoids in cannabis is Tetrahydrocannabinol (THC), the psychoactive element which causes the "high" sensation. It was discovered in 1964 by Dr. Raphael Mechoulam at Hebrew University in Israel.[49] To this day, Dr. Mechoulam is the preeminent scientist in the field of cannabis research.

The federal 2018 Farm Bill legalized Cannabidiol (CBD) derived from cannabis along with hemp. By law, CBD products must contain less than 0.3 percent THC. CBD is believed to have many health benefits. CBD exploded as an industry after its legalization. CBD and

THC are just two of the 113 cannabinoids found in cannabis.

There are three kinds of CBD: full-spectrum, broad-spectrum, and isolate. Full-spectrum CBD contains all the cannabinoids and essential oils of cannabis, including THC, but not enough to get you high. However, if used daily, it might contain enough to create a false positive on a drug test.[50] With full-spectrum CBD, users feel the "entourage effect," which enhances the health benefits one receives from the cannabinoids, terpenes, and flavonoids found in cannabis and CBD. Scientists have begun to prefer the term "ensemble effect" to describe what happens when someone consumes full-spectrum CBD because the cannabinoids work together, with all contributing something to achieving the desired effect rather than being led like an entourage.

Broad-spectrum is like full-spectrum but has the THC removed. It is also supposed to create the "entourage effect." Isolate CBD is supposed to be just CBD, with none of the other cannabinoids found in the plant. It goes through a winterization process that extracts everything that is not CBD. There are several forms in which CBD can be consumed, including capsules, oils, lotions, balms, foods, and beverages.

Another prominent cannabinoid is cannabinol (CBN), which is found in old cannabis and results from THC degrading over time. It is effective in addressing health problems such as inflammation, pain, bacteria, and helps with bone growth and increasing appetite.[51] A study on rodents said it helped decreased arthritis while another found it effective in addressing glaucoma.

Another cannabinoid identified is Cannabigerol (CBG), which can treat glaucoma in addition to addressing inflammation, slowing tumor growth, and killing strong strands of bacteria.[52] CBG does not have intoxicating effects, which makes it attractive to produce and market. CBG is created early in the development of the plant, and then mostly turns into other cannabinoids.

Thus, it is difficult and expensive to mass market as an isolate since only a small percentage is produced when the cannabis plant is harvested. A large number of plants are needed to extract a sufficient amount of CBG. In stark contrast, some strains of hemp contain 20 percent CBD. Because only a low percentage is available, expensive equipment is needed for extraction.

New applications are discovered each year, which brings us a new perspective on the remarkable cannabis plant. It is because cannabis research is in its infancy due to federal prohibition. That explains why THC was discovered in Israel and not the United States.

The Effects of Cannabis

Unlike alcohol and tobacco, cannabis cannot kill those who use it. There is no evidence that anyone has ever overdosed due to cannabis, unlike cocaine and heroin. Nor does it cause lung cancer like tobacco.[53] And in stark contrast to alcohol, it does not make users angry or violent, as Prohibitionists once suggested.

Furthermore, no proper medical study has stated that it causes mental illness. Mental illness might become conflated with cannabis use because the symptoms of a pre-existing mental illness might only become apparent around the time cannabis is consumed. People also try to self-medicate with cannabis.[54] Cannabis is currently being used by many to treat mental issues such as anxiety and depression. Several cannabis strains are effective in treating mood swings.[55]

However, cannabis use has caused excessive paranoia in some people, along with behaviors triggered by lowered inhibition. Paranoia usually occurs due to excessive consumption, while others may become awkward, or more forgetful. Driving after smoking cannabis should be avoided. You might become a little lazier. There is a stereotype that those who consume cannabis are lethargic. However, most people do not smoke before they do something that they are not inclined to do in the first place.

Pot brownies are the most difficult to dose for many because, unlike smoking, it takes much longer for the effects to occur. If someone does not feel the effects immediately and consumes another brownie, the feeling will be even stronger when it takes effect. The adage of "everything in moderation" should be applied to cannabis as well.

After smoking, a person will likely laugh more, eat a lot, which is known as "getting the munchies," and then fall asleep. Consuming cannabis generally causes one's mood to be lifted, induces feelings of euphoria, creativity, increases laughter, and appreciation of music.[56] One is more likely to consider abstract thoughts, but not likely at all to see hallucinogenic visuals.

A Rose by Any Other Name

Cannabis has many names including (but not limited to):

1. Marijuana
2. Mary Jane
3. Weed
4. Pot
5. Grass
6. Green
7. Herb
8. Trees
9. 420
10. Dope
11. Doobie
12. Mota[57]
13. Hemp
14. Indian Hemp
15. Skunk
16. Ganja

17. Chronic
18. Reefer
19. Mezz
20. Wacky Tobaccy

Every strain of cannabis is different. There are almost countless strains since growers are constantly developing new ones. Connoisseurs can tell the difference and describe the effects and taste of each strain in a detailed manner. They are beginning to prefer the term "cultivar" instead of "strain." Here is a list of well-known strains. It is by no means comprehensive:

1. Purple Haze
2. OG Kush
3. Pineapple Express
4. Blue Dream
5. Sour Diesel
6. Girl Scout Cookies
7. Gorilla Glue
8. White Widow
9. Durbin Poison
10. Grape Ape
11. Bubba Kush
12. AK 47
13. Gelato
14. Wedding Cake
15. Sunset Sherbet
16. Jack Herer
17. Bruce Banner
18. Godfather O.G.
19. Harlequin

20.   Maui Wowie[58]

How to Consume Cannabis

The most popular way people get high is to inhale smoke, hold it in their lungs, and blow the smoke out. However, there are different ways to smoke. One of the most important things to know about getting high is to "start low and go slow." Doctors and other medical professionals in the field often recommend this to patients. That means having a little bit over time and seeing how you like it, so you do not get too high. Set and setting are important also, meaning being in a familiar place among people you trust would be a good idea for your first time.

Because smoke can be harsh on one's lungs, some people prefer edibles. Edibles are especially popular in the legal markets. They get you high in a different way than smoking does. It takes at least 45 minutes to start feeling the effects. Edibles are often stronger, and its effects last longer than smoking. Consuming brownies infused with cannabis oil is immensely popular. Cannabis oil is also known as "tincture." Other desserts and snacks like cookies and rice treats can be baked. Gummies have become popular too. Gummies are problematic because lawmakers and prohibitionists say that children will eat gummies because they look like innocent candy. Thus, some have argued that laws should be passed to prevent the resemblance to gummy bears.[59]

There are also topicals creams, made from cannabis, designed to reduce pain. You cannot get high from these creams once you apply them because THC cannot be absorbed through the skin. Thus, they are only used for medical purposes.

Etiquette:

Etiquette is just as important among cannabis enthusiasts as it is among polite society. Showing proper etiquette will go a long way.

When enthusiasts gather, if one is friendly and warm, people will often share cannabis with the newcomer. So, it is important to observe the rules.

When the instrument of getting high is handed to you, take a deep inhalation, and hold it, then blow it out. It is ok if you cough; that is a natural reaction to smoking. You will likely get "cottonmouth," meaning your mouth is dry. It's good to have something to drink.

You can generally take two hits, and then you are expected to pass it, usually to the left. It is known as "Puff, Puff, Pass." Do not linger passing it or "sit on it." It can be seen as rude, even if one is distracted. It is known in some circles as "Bogarting." Also, do not accidentally put the lighter in your pocket. When putting your lips on the pipe or joint, try not to leave excess saliva.

Many use cannabis to self-medicate serious illnesses before consulting with a physician. It has been argued that all cannabis is medicine. Therefore, the term "recreational cannabis" is used sparingly throughout this book; it is referred to as "adult-use cannabis." Adult-use emphasizes the requirement that one must be at least 21 years old to consume any form of cannabis.

CHAPTER 3
HEMP

The hemp form of cannabis has the potential to revolutionize the economy. More farmers are turning to hemp cultivation because it is especially attractive for those looking for a lucrative and durable crop. In some states, it has become a booming industry. According to *Forbes*, the number of hemp farms in the United States quadrupled in 2019.[60]

Hemp, a member of the *Cannabis sativa* family, does not contain a sufficient amount of THC for recreational use. Instead, its stalks and seeds have been harvested for centuries to produce a wide array of products, including:

1. Paper[61]
2. Clothes[62]
3. Rope
4. Textiles
5. Building material[63]
6. Cars[64]
7. Fuel
8. Food[65]
9. Drinks

10. Health Supplements
11. Medicine
12. Treating polluted soil
13. Ship Sails
14. Paint
15. Plastic[66]
16. Soap
17. Batteries
18. Lotion
19. Medicine

Hemp forests offer a great solution to address climate change.[67] Hemp grows very quickly, far more quickly than normal trees. While a regular forest might take more than 20 years to mature, a field of hemp trees will grow to 13 feet tall in little more than three months, 100 days to be precise.[68] Thus, forests that were erased and would otherwise take far too long to grow can be replaced in less than a year with hemp forests. Also, hemp trees absorb the greenhouse gas carbon dioxide very efficiently.[69] While billions of acres might need to be planted, hemp growth is considered a feasible solution to a serious issue.

Hemp can be made into plastic with thousands of uses. Plastic is not environmentally friendly because it does not biodegrade. That means it will look largely the same after 100 years of being buried in the ground while hemp would rot and turn into soil. Also, one million birds die every year due to plastic.[70] Hemp can also be used to create the same products that are far more environmentally friendly than those derived from fossil-fuel based chemicals.

In contrast to the partisan rancor that has generally paralyzed Congress, hemp legalization and the emerging industry enjoy great bipartisan support. Legalization has long garnered Democratic Party support, especially from progressive members of the House of Representatives. But an increasing number of Republican Members of Congress have endorsed legalization. Even though hemp does not contain sufficient THC to get you high, it was included in the 1937 Marihuana Tax Act. Senate Majority Leader Mitch McConnell (R-KY) championed the 2018 Farm Bill that was signed into law that December. Hemp is a major cash crop in his native state of Kentucky. The 1942 war film "Hemp for Victory" described how well it grew there.

Geoffrey Whaling, chairman of the National Hemp Association (NHA), noted how much progress had been made fighting for hemp in the last few years.

"(In 2019) I stood earlier this year at USDA's crop and science conference and began by thanking them for hosting me, and I said I found it ironic when two years ago nobody here returned my calls," Whaling said. He reflected on the growing acceptance of hemp. Support comes from many farmers who are struggling and thus looking for an additional source of revenue, which makes hemp intriguing. Whaling said he went to a farming conference in the Midwest in 2019. His booth was constantly packed, not only with farmers who cultivate thousands of acres but also local politicians, agricultural officials, and bankers looking to seize the opportunity. Many family farms have histories of growing hemp, Whaling added.

"Many cotton growers used to grow hemp," he explained. Thus, elected officials with large rural constituencies and those who see the potential in hemp are supportive of the nascent industry.

"It's one of those topics that we don't get a lot of pushback ever," Whaling added. For example, Senator Cory Gardener (R-CO) is a strong backer of Colorado's cannabis and hemp markets. Many other Congressional Republicans selectively support cannabis-related bills, especially those from states where the industry is booming, like

McConnell's Kentucky.[71]

In the swing state of Florida, Governor Ron DeSantis (R) signed a bill into law in early 2019, asking the USDA permission to launch a hemp market in the state. Many farmers whose lands have been battered by hurricanes in past years are interested in growing hemp. Whaling noted that the Farm Bill of 2014, which allowed hemp research, laid the groundwork for broader support for the 2018 Farm Bill.

While a champion of hemp, McConnell remains opposed to the legalization of cannabis, calling it "hemp's illicit cousin." Many farmers who support hemp are also not in favor of adult-use cannabis.

"It's a generational thing. A younger generation has access to information from around the world and knows more about hemp and its potential than their parents or grandparents," Whaling said. This is true not only in hemp but adult-use cannabis as well. It is older individual who are most opposed to legalization.

While hemp was legalized on the federal level, regulations are in the nascent stages. The USDA stated that even though the U.S. Justice Department has not acted on the legislation, language in the Farm Bill gives the USDA the authority to deschedule hemp. That means they determined that it should no longer be included under the Controlled Substance Act (CSA), the federal drug policy that lists illegal drugs.[72] Cannabis is currently listed as a Schedule I drug, meaning the federal government thinks it has no medical use and is highly addictive. If it were descheduled and taken of the CSA, it would thus be legal.

In May 2019, the United States Department of Agriculture (USDA) announced that states cannot interfere with the interstate transportation of hemp, even if their respective state government has yet to legalize it.[73] They also stated that hemp could not be seized as illegal contraband. This is a serious issue in Idaho, where a truck transporting hemp was seized, and individuals were arrested for transporting hemp legally grown by their employer in Oregon. The drivers initially faced five years in jail.

"The USDA ruling provides even more support to our efforts to have our shipment returned," said Ryan Shore, CEO of Big Sky Scientific, the drivers' employer at the time. "We believe the Ninth Circuit Court of Appeals will rule in our favor and order release of our property." Their prosecution became exceedingly unpopular in Idaho.

"I think it's great," State Rep. Ilana Rubel, D-Boise, said of the USDA's ruling. "I hope that it is one more thing nudging the prosecutors to drop the charges."

More than 13,000 people signed a petition demanding the individuals be released. They have since been released and were ultimately convicted of misdemeanors and forced to pay high fees because while hemp is legal federally, it still has to be legalized on the state level in Idaho.[74]

The USDA clarified that Native American tribes must also allow transportation across their respective territories. However, tribes are still able to limit production within their jurisdictions. And while tribes can collaborate with states that have hemp research programs, they cannot authorize research programs themselves.

The USDA's announcement was expected to encourage more credit unions to assist hemp businesses, furthering the growth of an industry that was already booming. Shortly afterward, in 2019, the National Credit Union Administration (NCUA) announced they would allow credit unions to accept hemp businesses as clients since hemp was legalized.

"Lawful hemp businesses provide exciting new opportunities for rural communities," said NCUA Chairman Rodney Hood. "Many credit unions have a long and successful history of providing services to the agriculture sector. My expectation is that credit unions will thoughtfully consider whether they are able to safely and properly serve lawfully operating hemp-related businesses within their fields of membership."

The NCUA regulates, charters, and supervises federal credit unions. The federal agency published interim guidance for federally insured credit unions interested in providing service to legally operating hemp businesses.

"I'm delighted to hear the NCUA has answered my call on behalf of Kentuckians to ensure the legal hemp industry can access much-needed financial services," McConnell said. He noted that many individuals within the hemp industry complained about the difficulties they had in securing loans for their respective businesses. When regulations were not forthcoming, McConnell pushed for guidance on hemp banking, along with Sen. Michael Bennett (D-CO). Acquiring access to financial services has been an issue for hemp-related businesses for some time.

In their announcement, the NCUA highlighted the need for credit unions to comply with the Bank Secrecy Act (BSA) and Anti-Money Laundering (AML) to assure the federal government they are not doing business with anyone engaging in illegal practices. Previously, the BSA made credit unions and traditional banks hesitant to take on hemp businesses as clients.

CHAPTER 4

DECRIMINALIZATION

D ecriminalization of cannabis possession, and payment of a small fine instead of a lengthy jail sentence, has become increasingly pervasive across the country as a step on the way to full legalization. For decades, police have arrested countless individuals for possession. Twenty-seven states and Washington, DC have passed decriminalization of cannabis laws. The states that have approved decriminalization are marked with (D) while the states where cannabis is fully legal are marked with an (L):

1) Connecticut (D)
2) Delaware (D)
3) Hawaii (D)
4) Maryland (D)
5) Minnesota (D)
6) Mississippi (D)
7) Missouri (D)
8) Nebraska (D)
9) New Hampshire (D)
10) New Mexico (D)
11) New York (D)
12) North Carolina (D)
13) North Dakota (D)

14) Ohio (D)
15) Rhode Island (D)
16) Alaska (L)
17) California (L)
18) Colorado (L)
19) Illinois (L)
20) Maine (L)
21) Massachusetts (L)
22) Michigan (L)
23) Nevada (L)
24) Oregon (L)
25) Vermont (L)
26) Washington (L)
27) Virginia (D)

& Washington, DC (L)[75]

Several cities and counties have also decriminalized cannabis, including:

1. Philadelphia, PA[76]
2. Pittsburgh, PA
3. Bethlehem, PA[77]
4. Houston, TX
5. Milwaukee, WI
6. Green Bay, WI
7. Madison, WI
8. Kansas City, MO
9. Atlanta, GA
10. Miami, FL
11. Orlando, FL[78]

12. Tampa, FL
13. New Orleans, LA
14. Toledo, OH
15. Wichita, KS
16. Fayetteville, AR
17. Missoula County, MT
18. Jefferson County, AL

New York City passed a decriminalization bill in the 1970s, but many said it was not effective due to a loophole. The problem was that cannabis in public view remained a misdemeanor. Police could thus easily force individuals to empty their pockets to expose it and then arrest them. While cannabis-related arrests did decrease from the 1970s to 1990s, under former Mayor Rudy Giuliani, arrests went up again. They continued doing so under Michael Bloomberg until he was ordered by a federal judge to end "stop and frisk."[79]

The New York State Legislature decriminalized cannabis in June 2019 after it failed to pass adult-use legalization. The law went into effect on August 27, 2019, 60 days after it was approved. Under the bill, possession of small amounts is now punishable with fines rather than jail time. Offenders caught with possession of less than one ounce of marijuana are issued a ticket for $50. Those caught with between one and two ounces of cannabis are cited a ticket for $200. Anyone caught with more than two ounces, though, will be charged with a misdemeanor.

The law allows for the expungement or destruction of records for those with past low-level possession convictions. FBI records show that 360,000 individuals were arrested for cannabis possession in New York between 2008 and 2017.[80] It was estimated that the arrests of 24,400 individuals would be erased under the new law.

"Communities of color have been disproportionately impacted by laws governing marijuana for far too long, and today we are ending this injustice once and for all," New York Governor Andrew Cuomo said after signing the bill. "By providing individuals who have suffered the consequences of an unfair marijuana conviction with a path to have their records expunged and by reducing draconian penalties, we are taking a critical step forward in addressing a broken and discriminatory criminal justice process."

Cuomo pushed for full legalization in 2019. After unveiling his legalization plan, the governor formed a workgroup to write an adult-use cannabis bill that released a report showing the positive impacts of statewide legalization.[81] The New York Legislature tried to pass full legalization in 2019, but advocates failed to secure enough votes in the State Senate by their deadline in mid-June, just before the end of the legislature's session. Momentum was lost when Cuomo separated a deal on cannabis reform from the state's annual budget bill, which was the original plan to secure its passage. Thus, decriminalization was seen as a compromise.

"This law is an important step in righting decades of injustice caused by the state's current drug laws. By removing the barriers and stigma that come with these records, we clear the path for many New Yorkers to find a job, housing and go on to live successful and productive lives," said Assembly Speaker Carl Heastie (D). Some lawmakers in favor of decriminalization preferred it to legalization because they believe legalization would increase drug use and allow for corporate advertising to become prevalent.

Cuomo signaled his willingness to support cannabis legalization after a primary challenge from actress Cynthia Nixon in the 2018 gubernatorial primary, who campaigned ardently for full legalization. Before that, Cuomo was hesitant to support cannabis reform.

Decriminalization does not bring increased revenue to the state, nor can legitimate cannabis businesses be opened as in Colorado or Oregon, where cannabis is fully legal. Some legalization advocates believe that overzealous police officers would find ways around the decriminalization law to continue targeting minorities for arrest.

At the NORML conference of 2019 the sentiment "Al Capone would have liked decriminalization" was often repeated to argue in favor of full legalization. Al Capone sold bathtub gin, which was never illegal to possess, unlike cannabis. Many people stockpiled alcohol prior to the advent of alcohol prohibition. Alcohol prohibition was nowhere near as harsh as cannabis prohibition. There always exceptions to alcohol prohibition. For example, religious wine was still sold. Alcohol prohibition became such a joke there was no way it could not be repealed. A lot of drinking conventions today stem from alcohol prohibition. Cocktails were invented to mask the poor taste of poorly made alcohol.

While alcohol was associated with Germans who are well known for making beer and many were harmed by alcohol prohibition, in the manner that cannabis prohibition has been used to discriminate against Hispanics and Blacks.

There are some cannabis prohibitionists claim to favor decriminalization instead of legalization. In some situations, this has prevented both from passing.

"Police have historically found a way to work around the decriminalization of marijuana," said Erin George of Citizen Action of New York. She pointed out that decriminalization also leaves in place penalties for those coping with probation and immigration issues.

Some in New York believe Cuomo did not whip legislators sufficiently in the manner that he had done in the past for his initiatives. Legislators from Long Island remained opposed to full legalization, and thus decriminalization was passed as a compromise. New York's legislature meets from January to June, so the effort could not continue in the fall of 2019. If cannabis were legalized, sales could generate up to $4.1 billion in economic activity in New York.

North Dakota also decriminalized possession of small amounts of cannabis in 2019, after a bill that removes the possibility of jail time was signed into law by Republican Governor Doug Burgum. The decriminalization bill, HB 1050, passed the state legislature by a narrow margin. HB 1050 was introduced in the North Dakota House by Majority Caucus Leader Shannon Roers Jones (R) and Rep. Bernie Satrom (R), and in the Senate by Senators Jessica Unruh (R), Kristen Roers (R), and Jessica Myrdal (R).

North Dakota's cannabis law states that those caught with half an ounce or less of cannabis will have to pay a $1,000 fine yet serve no jail time for a first-time offense. Those caught with more than half an ounce of cannabis will be charged with only a misdemeanor. Possession of cannabis paraphernalia is treated as only a minor infraction. The law went into effect on August 1, 2019. Pro-reform advocates were pleased.

"This legislation is far from ideal, but it is a substantial step in the right direction," said Matthew Schweich, deputy director of the Marijuana Policy Project (MPP). "It is very encouraging to see a conservative state like North Dakota acknowledge and rectify the injustice of jailing people for possession of small amounts of marijuana."

The bill was signed into law on May 2, 2019, with little fanfare from the Governor's office and the state's legislative leadership. Medical marijuana was legalized in North Dakota in 2017 via referendum. In April 2019, Governor Burgum signed into law legislation that added a dozen new conditions that qualify for clinical cannabis. Before decriminalization, North Dakota had the sixth-highest amount of cannabis arrests in the nation. The law called for the state legislature to consider studying both the merits and drawbacks of legalizing recreational cannabis.

A referendum initiative in North Dakota in 2018 to fully legalize cannabis failed. It would have legalized the sale and use of recreational cannabis for those 21 and older but left the mechanism of subsequent regulation and taxation to be devised by the legislature at a later date. Advocates have launched a campaign for a more narrowly worded ballot referendum to pass in November 2020.

Virginia became the latest state to decriminalize cannabis in early 2020. After Democrats took control of both legislative chambers for the first time since the 1990s in the 2019 election, decriminalization became one of their priorities. The law passed with bipartisan support in both the Virginia State Senate and Assembly.

Under the law, those caught with less than an ounce of cannabis will merely have to pay a $25 fee. The law in Virginia previously said that possession was punishable with up to 30 days in jail and a maximum fine of $500. Provisions including a process for expungement and sealing of past cannabis-related convictions, were added at the last minute.[82] Notably, employers are barred from checking if an individual was convicted of cannabis possession.[83]

"A supermajority of Virginians have for many years opposed the continued criminalization of personal possession, and the legislature has finally taken action to turn public opinion into public policy," said Jenn Michelle Pedini, executive director of Virginia NORML. Governor Ralph Northam (D) was supportive of decriminalization passing, having campaigned on it, and called for its passage in a State of the Commonwealth speech.

Virginia currently has a strange, exceedingly limited medical program. Only CBD and THC-A are available for patients. The program is so limited that Virginia NORML does not consider it to be a true medical marijuana program.[84]

Further reform of cannabis laws in Virginia is possible. Governor Northam and Attorney General Mark Herring (D), who is running to succeed the term-limited Northam in 2021, have indicated they support creating a full medical marijuana program.[85] Herring and a few other legislators have said they want to push for adult-use; Northam has not commented on it.

House Majority Leader Charniele Herring (D) said the new

decriminalization law "will prevent low-level offenders from receiving jail time for simple possession while we move toward legalization in the coming years with a framework that addresses both public safety and equity in an emerging market."

Thus, Virginia will be an interesting state to watch for further cannabis reform in the future.

While decriminalization makes possession of cannabis a minor crime not punishable with jail time, akin to a parking ticket, the substance is not a legitimate commodity. Some ardent cannabis advocates believe this allows the black market to continue flourishing. It certainly does nothing to create a legitimate industry with good-paying jobs and steady revenue stream for cash-strapped governments.

CHAPTER 5

THE NATURE OF MEDICAL MARIJUANA

From its historical use as an effective medicine, cannabis as a medically accepted treatment was popularized in the 1970s. It is now an accepted treatment for several ailments. However, state by state classification for treatment varies by specific ailments. *Leafly* has excellent information on which state allows what condition.[86] The following is a list of some of the qualifying conditions across the country:

1. Anxiety
2. Autism
3. Epilepsy/Seizures
4. Depression
5. PTSD
6. Insomnia
7. Chronic Pain
8. Migraines
9. ALS
10. AIDS
11. Cancer
12. Crohn's disease

13. Ulcerative colitis
14. Multiple Sclerosis
15. Muscle Spasms
16. Severe Nausea
17. Parkinson's disease
18. Alzheimer's disease
19. Arthritis
20. Hepatitis C
21. Cachexia (wasting syndrome)

The process of getting a medical cannabis card varies state by state. In states like California and Oklahoma, it is easy to obtain a medical card. Almost any qualifying condition is sufficient. In other states, it is more difficult. In others, such as New Jersey, it can be expensive to register in the medical marijuana program. It previously cost about $300 to see the doctor, $100 for registration, and about $300 for an ounce of cannabis.[87] For someone using medical marijuana regularly in the manner of medicine, one ounce will not last long. Plus, it is not covered by insurance. But it can be deducted from one's income tax.

A medical marijuana card should be treated like a driver's license and kept in one's wallet. Some states allow patients from other states to purchase cannabis at their dispensaries in what is known as reciprocity. However, police in other states may not recognize a medical marijuana card from another state. These laws are constantly changing. So do your research before traveling.

Many doctors have shied away from prescribing a federally illegal substance once a state medical marijuana program is set in place. Some programs have grown in leaps and bounds after great stagnation due to politics. Implementation depends on the Governor seeking to implement it. So Democrat Jon Corzine was defeated for re-election to the Governorship of New Jersey to Chris Corzine signed the medical marijuana bill into law but Christie was very reluctant to implement it.

When one does go to a medical dispensary, patients usually just purchase cannabis similar to the type grown illegally. There are, of course, several variations in terms of edibles and gummies.

Epidiolex, produced by G.W. Pharmaceuticals, is the only cannabis-derived drug approved by the Food and Drug Administration (FDA) on the market. The FDA, which has been wary of CBD, approved Epidiolex in 2018 to treat seizures associated with epilepsy in infants, after a study led by Dr. Orin Devinsky.[88] Devinsky is a professor of neurology, neurosurgery, and psychiatry at the NYU Grossman School of Medicine and director of NYU Langone's

Comprehensive Epilepsy Center.

In contrast to other substances, the effects of cannabis are not well understood. The federal government has not been eager to allow it to be studied. The University of Mississippi is the only institution in the United States currently allowed to grow cannabis to study its medical benefits. The small supply of medical marijuana available has delayed academic research projects for years. Additionally, many scientists have criticized the exceedingly poor quality of the crop that the facility does grow.

Dr. Lester Grinspoon, a professor at Harvard University, was instrumental in establishing that cannabis could be used effectively as medicine. He passed in June 2020 at the age of 92. Grinspoon spent five decades studying cannabis and wrote 12 books on the subject, the most famous of which is "Marihuana Reconsidered." He wrote that cannabis prohibition was a political tool to suppress a harmless plant that had no psychiatric drawbacks. With his Ivy League respectability, the book made Grinspoon a leader of the nascent cannabis legalization movement.[89]

However, initially, he was wary of cannabis. Grinspoon believed in the old propaganda about the harms of its use before he began studying it. He was encouraged to study cannabis by his friend, noted astronomer Carl Sagan. Sagan was an enthusiastic proponent of cannabis. Sagan is by many as an early leader of legalization in his own right.

"He'd wave the joint in front of me, and reply, "Oh Lester, have a puff, it's not going to hurt you a bit, and you'll love it," Grinspoon recounted regarding Sagan in an interview. He wrote "Marihuana Reconsidered" after being goaded on by Sagan. Originally, he wanted to write about the detriments of cannabis use. However, he failed to find supporting hard data and changed his position.

His 1993 book "Marijuana: The Forbidden Medicine" made a case for the plant to be used as a medicine, calling it the best substance that could be used for this purpose. He was initially interested in the medical use of cannabis to treat his son Danny who had cancer. While it did not cure his cancer, cannabis greatly helped ease Danny's pain from chemotherapy.

"On a normal day of chemotherapy," Grinspoon said, "I hoped we could make it home from the hospital before Danny's vomiting would start, and we always had to put a big bucket next to his bed. But the first time he tried taking a few puffs prior to a round of treatments, he got off the gurney and said, 'Mom, there's a sub shop in Brookline. Could we stop for a sub-sandwich on the way home?' And all I thought was, 'Wow.' Grinspoon's work led to a study that concluded officially that cannabis helped those suffering from the negative effects of chemotherapy, particularly nausea and vomiting.

After studying cannabis, Grinspoon became a great proponent of legalization and served on the board of NORML for years. His time as chair in the 1990s is credited with expanding the group after it had fallen on difficult times. As a legalization advocate, he testified before many congressional and state legislative committees on cannabis.

Being an early cannabis proponent had its drawbacks. While Grinspoon spent his entire career at the Harvard Medical School, he was twice passed over for a promotion due to his stance on cannabis.

Some medical marijuana programs, which started as both prohibitively expensive and treating only a minimum number of ailments, with few dispensaries selling medical marijuana, have improved over time. There is widespread consensus that the medical marijuana program in New Jersey under former Governor Chris Christie was designed to be ineffective. The medical marijuana law, the Compassionate Use of Medical Marijuana Act (CUMMA), was passed in the waning days of his predecessor, Jon Corzine. Under Christie, the New Jersey Department of Health (DOH) imposed education requirements on doctors who participated and required training courses in addiction pain management. It was unpopular, and few did so. Only 1,000 physicians signed up out of the 28,000 registered doctors in the state.

Governor Phil Murphy signed a law expanding the program in New Jersey in July 2019 to accommodate more patients and allow more dispensaries. New Jersey previously had one of the country's most restrictive programs. Many people complained about the lack of variety of available products, the price to enter the program, and the poor quality of the cannabis that is sold, which sometimes contains seeds. Cannabis with seeds is generally weaker.

Murphy also signed into law the Jake Honig Act, a bill inspired by a child with brain cancer who was not able to obtain the medicine needed to mitigate the pain and has since passed. Ken Wolski, Executive Director of the Coalition for Medical Marijuana in New Jersey (CMMNJ), was at the forefront of the fight for that bill and felt that a great victory was won.

"There are lots of good things in the bill. It allows caregivers to obtain medical marijuana for patients. And physician's assistants and advanced practice nurses can prescribe medical marijuana now," Wolski said. Hospitals are also allowed to obtain clinical cannabis for patients in long-term care. However, they will be disinclined to do so if they are receiving funds from the federal government because it might cause them to lose that funding. Many do indeed receive federal funds.

One major merit of the bill is that patients must visit their doctor once a year for authorization instead of the previous four times. They will also be able to obtain three ounces a month versus two. Also, hospice and terminal patients will have no limit on the amount they can obtain monthly. In the past, those who could not obtain enough legal medical marijuana purchased the remainder they needed from the black market.

Edibles will be available for adults now in addition to minors who previously had access. Previously minors had access, but adults did not. Edibles include tinctures and oils that contain marijuana used in baking or cooking. Also included in the bill for patients were work and housing protections against discrimination. Clinical cannabis use will not interfere with child custody cases anymore. Out-of-state patients, though, can only obtain medical marijuana after receiving approval from an in-state physician, for up to six months.

One of the most significant aspects of the Jake Honig Act is that it permitted the issuance of new dispensary licenses. There were initially only six dispensaries throughout the state. Competition for a license to open one is fierce. Generally, those who are best poised to obtain a license are those with deep pockets and operations from out of state. But the bill set aside micro licenses for women and minority-owned businesses who seek to create small businesses. It also allowed dispensaries to deliver medicine to the patient's homes, which helps patients with limited mobility.

The tax on medical marijuana is considered sizeable by some activists. While the law largely phases out the state tax by 2022, a two percent dispensary tax collected by municipalities was designed to make dispensaries more welcome.

"About the only downside is there is no home cultivation. It's a real disappointment," Wolski said. "We will continue to pursue it for its affordable access and the therapeutic act of gardening. It gives you twice the bang for your buck."

He also noted that half of the states that have medical marijuana programs have also legalized cultivation as part of it. Another provision he criticized was the creation of a Cannabis Regulatory Commission.

"The DOH is good already. Why create another bureaucracy? The benefit is having it laying the groundwork for recreational adult cannabis," Wolski noted. As of June 2020, New Jersey had about 77,000 medical patients with a population of about nine million. Michigan also has about 9 million residents and had about 261,989 patients as of March 2020. Ohio has 11 million residents and 94,536 patients.[90]

Jay Lassiter is a long-time advocate for cannabis and LGBT rights in New Jersey, having fought for medical marijuana for years.

"I'll give Phil Murphy some credit. It has become easier to get into the program," he said after the Jake Honig Act passed. "But even that has its side effects. It has made the lines longer when that was always an issue." Lassiter said it was almost like going backward.

Cannabis policy and politics have changed greatly since Lassiter first became involved. The first rally he went to was organized by a guy he liked where the attendees were mainly HIV positive.

"Pot rallies in the early 90s centered on the AIDs crisis," Lassiter said. It was a direct response to the sick and dying queer. Dead queers gave us medical marijuana in America," he said.

Lassiter went to California in the mid-1990s, where medical marijuana was gaining popularity. He was a great fan of medical marijuana leader Dennis Peron's dispensary in San Francisco. At the time, Peron's dispensary helped many patients who had adverse reactions from the primitive AIDS drugs available at the time.

After the state referendum passed, there were few regulations on California's medical program. The federal government did not believe the state had the authority to legalize cannabis. Thus, many dispensaries were raided by the police and the DEA. Lassiter was at Peron's dispensary when it was raided once.

"I was there because I wanted to make sure I was stocked up," Lassiter said. "It was where society's rejects hung out and felt fellowship and company. A lot of people were very sick," he explained.

It was the political action of the gay LGBT people and their allies, together with the AIDS crisis, that Lassiter credited with making cannabis a legitimate medical source. June became LGBT pride month in recognition of the Stonewall Riots in June 1969 in New York City's Greenwich Village. The riots kicked off the movement, which subsequently grew dramatically. The first gay pride march was the following June in 1970, making June 2020 the 50th anniversary of these events.

After years of advocacy, Lassiter is now a well-known writer for InsiderNJ.com. Lassiter said one of his accomplishments is simply living after being HIV positive for 28 years. The legalization of clinical cannabis in the Compassionate Use of Medical Marijuana Act (CUMMA) was great for him to be part of, after having advocated for its passage for so long.

In addition, seeing civil unions implemented was a great step forward on the way to marriage. A couple of years later, Lassiter went to Ireland two weeks before gay marriage was approved via referendum. He spent much of his vacation campaigning and logged many miles walking. Seeing Maryland, where he grew up, approve gay marriage was also an accomplishment. Lassiter went to Maryland after Hurricane Sandy and served as a county Field Director when gay marriage was on the ballot. It was the first time that gay marriage was approved by a referendum and the first win after several losses.

"It's nice my friends aren't dying of AIDS anymore," Lassiter said, reflecting on the meaning of (June) Pride Month. "Nowadays, it's a chance to hang out and get a chance to spend time with friends."

He noted that pride events are often family-friendly with playground arrangements.

"You never would have dreamed of that 20 years ago," Lassiter said. He noted it has become an event where politicians seeking support often visit.

But overall, cannabis advocacy has not been full of easy victories. Lassiter noted as others have, cannabis advocacy is difficult.

"(It's been) mostly a lot of low lows because lawmakers are pretty much awful people. They never fail to disappoint," Lassiter said.

After many years of fighting, Lassiter is unhappy about the medical marijuana program in New Jersey.

"New Jersey gets none of my business. I usually go to a dispensary in another state," he said. Lassiter lives in Cherry Hill, NJ, near Philadelphia. He said he smokes to cope with the great anxiety caused by the Trump era.

Lassiter said it is a lot easier to become a patient in other states. He blames many of the regulations left over from the former governor Chris Christie era.

"I'm just glad to have a black-market contact," he said regarding his source of cannabis.

He is fully in favor of decriminalization to address the issue of patients turning elsewhere. Lassiter noted that in 2018, New Jersey Attorney Gurbir Grewal called for an end to the prosecution of cannabis crimes. That stoppage was short-lived.

Like many other long-time cannabis advocates, Lassiter laments the lack of homegrow in New Jersey. The other major issue in the medical program was the lack of home delivery at the time. Lassiter called the system the "cartel model."

"The regulations allow the dispensaries to be greedy and forces them to have high prices, due to overhead," Lassiter said. He added dispensaries have burdensome rules to follow. For example, they need to destroy unsold pieces of cannabis.

"We are fighting for home delivery during a crisis, a pandemic when we are trying to keep medically fragile people at home," Lassiter added. He noted regulations have already been bent for COVID-19. Telemedicine for incoming medical marijuana patients was implemented by emergency regulation, for example.

"It's really maddening," Lassiter lamented.

"Sometimes it feels like, oh my God, I can't believe how much progress we've made! Other times it feels like it's taken forever," Lassiter said, reflecting on the journey. "Sometimes, even on the same day. "It's rewarding and challenging still," he said.

The use of medical marijuana is slowly spreading from blue states to redder areas of the country. For example, Oklahoma has a robust medical marijuana program, even though their referendum was only approved in 2018. It benefits nearly 250,000 patients, or 6.3 percent of the state's population in spring 2020.[91]

In Oklahoma, all doctors can prescribe clinical cannabis to treat a variety of conditions. Moreover, towns cannot pass laws banning dispensaries within their city limits, so there are many throughout the state. In stark contrast, other states allowed conservative towns to ban medical dispensaries within their limits. Thus, few are located in politically conservative regions in many states.

There is no cap on the number of licenses in Oklahoma and few barriers to entry, unlike other states where the opposite is true. It also took other states many years to arrive at the present level of patients in their medical marijuana programs.

Utah also approved medical marijuana by referendum in November 2018. However, the Church of Jesus Christ of Latter-Day Saints, or the Mormon Church, opposed the measure. The Mormon Church, founded in the 19th century, wields enormous power in Utah. Most of its leaders since its founding have been Mormons, including the current Governor, both U.S. Senators, and 90 percent of the state legislature. Governor Gary Herbert, a Republican, came out strongly against the referendum, claiming to have met individuals in recovery who said that marijuana was their gateway drug. Conversely, former Senator Orrin Hatch (R-Utah), a Mormon himself, endorsed the idea of medical marijuana.

In an example of their power, in 2017, the Church backed a bill which lowered drunk driving blood alcohol limits to 0.05 percent, the lowest level in the country by far. That bill passed. Officially the church cannot tell its members to vote against the initiative because doing so would threaten the generous benefits it receives as not-for-profit organization. The state was one of the first to ban cannabis in the early 1900s.

Legalization first became popular in more progressive Democratic states, such as California. Now that Utah's swing-state neighbors of Colorado and Nevada have legalized cannabis, it is natural the fight would spill over to Utah.

The church requires devout members to abstain from alcohol, tobacco, coffee, tea, and "illegal drugs." Therefore, they do not allow parishioners to be married in a Mormon church if they are known to be using marijuana, even if they are suffering from severe medical conditions. In April 2018, the Church endorsed a letter written by the Utah Medical Association denouncing supporters of the ballot measure who are using it to "disguise their true aim... paving a way for recreational use of cannabis in Utah." The church joined with law enforcement associations saying that the bill would "compromise the health and safety of Utah communities" in addition to creating "significant challenges to law enforcement."[92]

Mormons in states where marijuana is legal who use it for medicinal purposes are in good standing with their local churches. While 60 percent of Utah is Mormon, two-thirds support the ballot measure's passage.

Many supporters of the referendum touted its benefits to patients as an alternative to far more dangerous opioid drugs, which, in addition to being severely addictive, cause many people to lose their energy. According to a study by the University of California, San Diego, hospitalization rates for opioid painkiller dependence and abuse have fallen 23 percent, and hospitalization for opioid overdoses has dropped 13 percent in states where medical cannabis has been legalized by 2018.[93] Proponents of the law often emphasized the positive results that veterans seeking to cope with severe PTSD have had when using medical marijuana elsewhere.

Ultimately, the Utah referendum passed. However, shortly afterward, with the Mormon Church's backing, the Utah legislature passed a bill that overrode the referendum and enacted a far stricter clinical cannabis program that allowed fewer conditions and far fewer dispensaries, among other issues.[94] Proponents of clinical cannabis essentially said it was better than nothing.

Even in the older medical marijuana programs, the nuances are being fine-tuned. In October 2019, California passed a bill that gave school boards the authority to allow parents to give their children medical marijuana on the grounds of public K-12 schools. An increasing number of children and teenagers in California and other states with legal medical marijuana use it to treat a variety of conditions, the most common being seizures. The bill was named "Jojo's Act" after Jojo Garcia, a high school student who needs daily doses of cannabis oil to control his seizures. Previously, students who are registered medical marijuana patients had to leave campus to have the cannabis administered.

"Jojo's Act would enable students who are living with severe medical disabilities and rely on medicinal cannabis to take their medication on campus under strict conditions and supervision, so they can get on with their school day without disrupting their education," said State Sen. Jerry Hill (D-San Mateo), the bill's sponsor.[95]

Jojo's mother, Karina, had to come in the middle of the school day to administer the oil to her son, at least 1,000 feet away from school. Another parent who testified before the State Senate shared that the rule had caused her child to miss 10 percent of class time in total.

"I was watching my son die right before my eyes," she said regarding her son's condition before using medical marijuana. "It is not fair that this medicine that has saved my son's life [would] not be given the same treatment as other pharmaceuticals on campus."

The bill only allowed non-smoking forms of oils, pills, and lotions to be administered to children by their parents. The California School Boards Association endorsed the bill's passage, saying in a letter to lawmakers, "Every child is entitled to an uninterrupted education."

Former Gov. Jerry Brown (D) vetoed a similar bill in 2018, noting that it was "too broad." Republicans in California's legislature, law enforcement groups, and anti-legalization advocates opposed Jojo's

Act. They did not see cannabis as a legitimate medicine and felt it would somehow allow recreational drugs on school property.

Republican lawmakers noted that California has a broad definition of what ailments can be treated by medical marijuana. The program allows doctors to recommend medical cannabis for any condition or symptom. Thus, California is one of the easiest states in which to obtain a medical card. State lawmakers are now considering whether to provide the same protections to veterinarians who recommend cannabis to pets.

"No one has ever been denied a recommendation," complained state Sen. Andreas Borgias (R-Modesto). Similar school medical marijuana bills have been approved in Colorado, Illinois, Washington, Maine, Delaware, New Jersey, Florida, and New Mexico.

The education of law enforcement about medical marijuana cannabis has been a long process. Because some did not learn quickly enough, Brian Powers had his day in court for his alleged crime in January 2020. Powers was arrested in New Brunswick, New Jersey, in November 2019 for cannabis possession. However, he is a patient who had his medical marijuana card and cannabis from an Alternative Treatment Center (ATC) with him at the time. A Middlesex County sheriff's deputy arrested him while he was smoking from a pipe on the sidewalk outside the county courthouse. He had been in the area working and stepped outside for a quick smoke, walked a block, and found himself in trouble even though this was perfectly legal.

Powers was charged with possession felonies, along with obstruction of justice for spitting on the officer. His medical marijuana was bought from Garden State Dispensary near his home and was in its properly labeled container when he was arrested. Ultimately, he was held for three hours and then released. Powers said if he had his camera, he would have filmed it and not been arrested since the cop would have been afraid of looking bad. Powers denied deliberately spitting on the officer. It was speculated that spittle might have been accidentally expelled while he was speaking.

After initially having his case transferred to New Brunswick municipal court from Middlesex County court, his medical marijuana crime charges were dropped along with the threat of jail time under a felony. He still had to fight a disorderly conduct charge another day in a formal trial. The defendant maintained he is not guilty.

Powers had been an official medical patient in the NJMMP program for a year for anxiety and depression by the time he was arrested. It's something he had been seeking treatment for since he was in his 20's with little success. However, he experienced great improvement since beginning to use clinical cannabis.

He had sought to represent himself in the case and get the charges dropped quickly. Powers had consulted a lawyer for advice on the matter before going to court. The judge advised him going forward to get a proper lawyer, saying if she had to file a motion for discovery on the case, she would have to hire a lawyer to do so as well. He was not happy about the situation.

"Throw the father of five children in jail because a pig doesn't know the law," Powers said regarding the case. "This whole fucking system is run by pigs. I got a living to make and because a pig doesn't know the law, so now I'm out money and time?"

"Make a living off of poor people's blood, that's what they do," Powers added. He is a family man with five sons who works as a Labor Organizer. Also, he has a company called NJ Revolution Radio, which produces podcasts.

His business partner Heather Warburton posted on Facebook that "Tomorrow my friend and business partner Brian is going to court to defend himself against criminal charges connected to possessing cannabis. He is a medical patient and still had his medicine in the bag from the dispensary. The pigs in New Brunswick didnt (sic) care about things like the law. They saw a long-haired hippie sitting on a bench smoking weed and decided their feelings were more important than anything else. They handcuffed him and shoved him into a wall. Feel free to call the Middlesex County Prosecutor and ask why they are harassing sick people trying to use their completely legal medication."

According to Powers, he had at least four messages on Facebook that people had done so.

Sativa Cross, led by Edward "Lefty" Grimes, joined Powers in New Brunswick to give him moral support. Lefty was also trying to get arrested outside the courthouse with his friend and fellow activist Michelle Burns as an act of civil disobedience. She has Multiple Sclerosis (MS) and needs an electronic wheelchair to get around. In the cold weather, Burns was trying to get arrested for lighting her joints by the courthouse. Lefty filmed her while officers were entering the county courthouse. However, Burns did not succeed. Powers said they learned from his experience.

"I helped train pigs," Powers declared. "I'm the pig whisperer."

Powers was ultimately acquitted of all crimes and received his cannabis, pipe, and grinder back.

Thus, laws and practices are slowly getting changed to accommodate patients. The New Jersey State Supreme Court ruled in March 2020 that medical marijuana patients cannot get fired for testing positive for cannabis.

"This protects hundreds, if not thousands of employees" who've faced the "stigma of marijuana," said Jamison Mark, a lawyer for Justin Wild, the plaintiff who is a former funeral director.[96]

Wild was using medical marijuana to treat the effects of cancer. In 2016, he was in a car accident through no fault of his own, and his Ridgewood-based funeral home employer demanded that he take a drug test. Wild was fired when the drug test came back positive, and he subsequently sued based on discrimination.

Ideally, the case *Justin Wild. v. Carriage Funeral Holdings Inc.* will set a precedent and benefit those who must cope with a drug test deemed mandatory at work. Patients now have better protection against discrimination in the workplace. The Court noted that just because the Compassionate Use of Medical Marijuana Act (CUMA) does not explicitly say patients are protected in the workplace, the existing Law Against Discrimination (LAD) on the state level gives them that protection.

"Today was an important victory for employees throughout New Jersey who use medical marijuana. ... our Supreme Court affirmed the appellate division's holding that those who are terminated from their jobs, based upon their proper medical use of marijuana, may bring a disability discrimination claim under the Law Against Discrimination," said Dillon McGuire. He argued on behalf of the Americans for Civil Liberties Union (ACLU) of New Jersey.

It is key to note that the use of cannabis did not impair Wild from carrying out his job. Unfortunately, he was still unemployed and looking for work within the funeral industry when the case was decided in March 2020. Drug tests are just one of the issues that patients in New Jersey cope with as prohibition continues.

Initially, a lower court sided with the funeral home, which forced Wild and his lawyer to appeal to the State Supreme Court. (The State Supreme Court is the highest state court level in New Jersey. In New York, the highest level is called the Court of Appeals.).

"The court's decision today was an important step toward securing the rights and dignity that medical marijuana patients deserve," Maguire said. Wild has another lawsuit against his employer that will proceed in Bergen Superior Court.

In November 2019, Amazon fired a worker in one of their New Jersey warehouses for a positive drug test even though he was in the medical marijuana program.[97] Not only was the man fired from that warehouse, but he was also blacklisted from working at other Amazon-owned entities, such as Whole Foods. The man was using clinical cannabis to treat anxiety disorder.

In general, the more white-collar a job is, the lower the likelihood is that you will be drug tested. Thus, it seems those who work in blue-collar positions are less trusted. Employers say physically demanding jobs dictate that workers be alert. Drug testing at work has increased by 277 percent since 1987. One reason drug testing persists is that it helps companies obtain better insurance rates in some cases. Others like the idea of touting themselves as anti-drug.[98] The people who are hurt by this type of discrimination are the working class and most vulnerable.

CHAPTER 6

THE POSITIVE EFFECTS OF MEDICAL MARIJUANA ON PATIENTS

Many people have used medical marijuana to treat severe conditions. It has allowed them to go from being near bedridden to continuing as vibrant members of their communities. Jessie Gill is one of these.

The founder of Marijuana Mommy, she has made a national name for herself in the cannabis industry as a nurse educating people on the benefits of the plant. Initially, Gill was a hospice nurse who worked hard to maintain her health and an active lifestyle. However, a work-related spinal injury caused her to experience severe pain for a long while. Traditional western medicine gave her little respite from the pain, though she was taking up to 15 pills a day, including opiates that left her barely functioning and desperate. The extent of her pain illuminates the limitations of traditional health care.

When a friend suggested she try cannabis, she was exceedingly hesitant to do so. Being trained as a nurse in western medicine, Gill was not aware of documented cases highlighting the medical benefits of cannabis. The stereotype of the "lazy stoner" made her disinclined to do so. Using cannabis as a mother was initially scary.

"The stigma is still strong on the East Coast, and people's judgments can have concrete consequences," she said. Also, she had a bad experience trying it for recreational purposes when younger.

However, with nowhere else to turn, Gill became a medical marijuana patient. The pain largely subsided, and she began to be able to live a normal life. After becoming a medical marijuana patient, Gill stopped taking all the prescriptions that did little to ease her suffering and left her mind feeling cloudy.

When she told her children that she was using cannabis, their reactions differed. Gill said her daughter, who was a teenager at the time, was surprised and apprehensive but was very supportive, especially after seeing how much medicinal cannabis helped her. Her son was only in the third grade, so explaining it to him was different.

"He didn't understand what marijuana was and hadn't been exposed to much prohibition. I had to prepare him for the negative stigma and myths he was going to face in school," she said. And while there is a perceived stigma, Gill happily noted she did not face any backlash over becoming a patient.

The utter reversal of her life from great despair and illness to hope and health made Gill into an evangelist for cannabis. And from being ill and depressed, she is now a thriving, vivacious woman. There are many like Gill, who went from barely functioning due to pain and pills to lively community leaders.

As a proponent of cannabis, Gill created the website Marijuana Mommy as a resource to teach patients and consumers, and to challenge the stigma surrounding cannabis. Given that she had not been educated about its benefits while training to be a nurse, she expected others had similar notions.

While some might call her "Marijuana Mommy," she does not see it as her identity, but rather introduces herself as "the founder of Marijuana Mommy." The name Marijuana Mommy was first suggested by her daughter's college friend when Gill became involved in the cannabis field. She added that "My love of the name was also inspired by my mom, who's loving guidance encouraged me to become a cannabis patient. That's what I hope to offer patients via

MarijuanaMommy.com, loving guidance for what can seem like a scary topic."

The medical community has been slow to embrace the existence of the Endocannabinoid System, a human body function that benefits from cannabis use. However, Gill said some medical professionals have been open to learning about the benefits of cannabis. In contrast, others have entrenched negative beliefs from old propaganda.

Gill is a recognizable face in cannabis industry circles, having spoken at many conferences. Her writings have been featured in many prominent publications as well. She said about her notoriety that "it's crazier than anything I could have dreamed." Gill added that "it means the most to me when my work or story is featured in the mainstream media. The people who need me the most aren't reading industry publications or searching Google for cannabis info."

Gill is optimistic regarding the future of cannabis, saying that "federal legalization is inevitable. It's just a matter of time. We need it so badly. It'll increase access for patients everywhere and open the market to so many new consumers."

Leo Bridgewater is another example of someone whose use of cannabis changed his life. He is a prominent cannabis activist and businessman with a presence in the cannabis industry across the country, having consulted businesses in multiple states. Born and raised in Trenton, New Jersey, he joined the military in response to 9/11. Bridgewater was deployed to Iraq and Afghanistan as a telecommunications specialist. After deployment, he began having issues. He began using cannabis to treat his own PTSD and then began speaking with other veterans.

"Cannabis has allowed me to go from suffering from PTSD to living with PTSD, and I'm able to remain functional. It also allows me to, helps me to deal with pain in my knees," he said.

PTSD wasn't initially a qualifying condition in New Jersey's medical marijuana program, and Bridgewater fought with others to get the bill passed. He testified before the Assembly, and former Governor Chris Christie finally added PTSD to the list of qualifying conditions in 2016.

"The veteran voice is a very powerful voice if deployed right," he noted.

As a cannabis activist, he is on the board of Minorities 4 Medical Marijuana (M4MM) as the National Director for Veteran's Outreach. Bridgewater is also the co-founder of Leaf Launch Holdings. He also sits on the board of the Cannabis World Congress (CWC) and spoke at their expo in New York City in June 2019.

Bridgewater is optimistic about the eventual success of the industry and the movement, pointing to former Vice President Joe Biden's retraction of his comments calling cannabis a "gateway drug" on the presidential campaign trail in 2019.[99] He added that the high number of patients in the MMJ program and those concerned with social justice would continue to grow to become a voting bloc that could hurt incumbents in otherwise comfortable positions. Bridgewater believes this would then give the politicians opposed to legalization pause to think.

A new cannabis strain was released in May 2020 by Harmony dispensary in Secaucus, NJ, named BridgeH20 after Bridgewater. He said it had been a year and a half in the making.

"I want to name a strain after you," Harmony CEO Shaya Brodchandel said to him one day. Brodchandel added that many people had come into the dispensary saying the only reason they had decided to get their medical marijuana card was that they had heard Bridgewater speak.

"We knew we had to honor him as a veteran and cannabis advocate by collaborating with him on his very own strain," said Harmony Dispensary Director of Cultivation, Adam Johnstone.

"I was flattered," Bridgewater said.

Bridgewater has known Brodchandel for about four years through industry circles and events through which they have become close. Bridgewater spoke well of him, saying he was one of the few dispensary entrepreneurs that does a lot of community outreach.

While honored and flattered, he would never go through the process again.

"I wasn't prepared for the emotional roller coaster. I thought people grew, and they just throw your name on the shit," Bridgewater said.

He became an advocate for cannabis after realizing it would help him cope with his PTSD from his tour in Iraq.

"I found out I had triggers I didn't even know about," Bridgewater said about the process. It involved a great deal of trial and error and recording his reactions, feeling, and mood after every strain was tried.

Bridgewater said he has heard from contacts on the West Coast and Florida that want to sell his strain in the future.

"It's the ultimate industry nod. I know a whole bunch of people don't know who Jack Herer is, but they know his strain," Bridgewater said. As previously noted, Herer was a well-known hemp activist who wrote "The Emperor Has No Clothes."

Harmony currently only has one location in Secaucus, NJ.

"The industry reaction has been absolutely phenomenal," Bridgewater said.

The BridgeH20 cannabis strain is a hybrid that is 70/30 Indica combining the strains Wedding Cake, Chemdog, and OG.

"I lean towards a heavy Indica so that I don't dream," Bridgewater explained. He often has nightmares that leave him more tired when he wakes than when he went to sleep. It was almost physically demanding, he said. The strain they came up with is quite strong even for a veteran smoker like Bridgewater. He admitted trying it made him feel like a novice smoker.

"Do not consume bridgeh20 and then have someplace to go. This is your nightcap," Bridgewater advised.

Bridgewater said that it has a unique, welcoming dank aroma that is piney.

"I slept for 10 hours," he said. The cannabis strain was strong; it seemed he woke up the next day and forgot he had smoked it.

The day after smoking it, he felt much better. He said that he felt rested and that his mood was enhanced. While feeling enhanced, he was much more productive than he otherwise would have been.

"I sent Adam a message. You hit this one out of the park!" Bridgewater said.

Bridgewater was curious how his brand-new cannabis strain would work when making an edible. He explained that due to the taste of strains, not every strain goes with every type of food.

"You can't just put AK-47 butter on some cornbread. The taste of the strain will not work with cornbread," Bridgewater explained. "It's all about taste and terpenes."

He recommended that people seek to appreciate its taste due to terpenes. When you have a legal cannabis market, one can be a connoisseur comparable to the way nuances of wine are critiqued and appreciated by aficionados. Strains can be appreciated for their special properties. Bridgewater added that this requires a degree of sophistication and experience smoking. He recommended that users experiment first with different dishes.

Laura Lagano says CBD worked to treat her daughter Isabella's autism. As a registered dietician and cannabis consultant, she is trained to understand the role of integrative food and nutrition in improving an individual's health.

With its potential to effectively manage health conditions, Western medicine has struggled to address cannabidiol (CBD) as its use has exploded. Among other uses, CBD is especially beneficial in helping children with autism, a condition that severely impairs an individual's ability to communicate and socialize.

Lagano, who believes autism is a confluence of symptoms that affect the whole body rather than merely a neurological disorder, has employed "alternative options for Isabella since she was four and now, she's 23," she said.

Initially, pharmaceutical drugs made Isabella's behavior worse. By the time she was four, she was on three medications. So Lagano took action and began including CBD in Isabella's regimen by adding it to smoothies.

"My daughter took me on this journey," Lagano says. "She's the reason why I decided to explore cannabis. Motherhood is a bumpy ride."

Isabella began having seizures that sometimes lasted for 50 minutes when she was just nine months old. Typically, they were quick. CBD quelled Isabella's anxiety, increased her ability to focus, and helped improve her language skills (which were impaired due to apraxia). Lagano emphasized that a one-size-fits-all approach regarding diet and CBD doesn't work. Results differ from person to person. CBD is not known for treating speech issues. So Lagano considers this a pleasant side-effect. Even with her health regime, Isabella was in an intense speech therapy program several days a week while growing up.

Many clinical testimonials point to the benefit of using CBD to treat health conditions. In 2018, a study conducted in Israel found that 80% of the children participating benefited from using CBD to treat their autism-derived symptoms. Disruptive behavior, communication issues, anxiety, and stress were all reduced by varying degrees. However, the CBD used in the study contained 1.5% THC, while CBD is only legal in the United States when it has 0.3 percent THC.

To legally obtain CBD with such a high amount of THC, parents of children with autism have to register them as medical marijuana patients to obtain it at a medical dispensary. Autism is not a qualifying condition in New Jersey for medical marijuana, though anxiety is.

"I enjoy my mother helping me with my food and supplements because I feel better," Isabella said. "When I take CBD, I feel less anxiety. It helps me throughout my day."

Along with CBD, a nutrition-focused food plan led to vast improvements in Isabella's condition.

"She loves to socialize and is very personable," Lagano proudly reported. "She's always loved people."

Lagano emphasized that a one-size-fits-all approach concerning diet and CBD doesn't work, and results differ from person to person. She's also adamant in her belief that people seeking to treat a medical condition are best assisted by a medical professional.

"Autism is a whole-body disorder impacting the gastrointestinal and neurological systems," Lagano, who co-founded the Holistic Cannabis Academy, concluded. "It's no surprise that cannabis impacts autism. This ancient plant can change the lives of individuals with special needs."

Jeff Oakes, a long time-activist with Sativa Cross, is one of the leading figures in New Jersey's legalization movement. A new effort to pass home cultivation or "homegrow" by advocates has been dubbed "Jeff's Law" in his honor. He only has a short time to live. Oakes is a cancer patient who was been deemed terminal with three to nine months of life left as of February 2020. His daughter graduated from college in May 2020. His goal was to be alive to see it. Oakes initially received his medical marijuana card to treat arthritis in July 2014. He then needed it for cancer, which he was diagnosed with in January 2016. It has helped him immensely.

"Cannabis is the only reason I eat at all and am able to keep weight on. It's the only way I could get past all these surgeries and radiation," Oakes said.

Oakes said he got cancer from his career in welding stainless steel that contained Hexavalent Chromium. Unfortunately, it is not uncommon in welding. He only received a letter regarding the hazard and a protective hood two years before being diagnosed. Oakes has had a legal case regarding this, which has dragged out since he was diagnosed. He has since become a proponent of clean energy in stark contrast to the fossil fuel facilities where he used to work.

Initially, Oakes was diagnosed with colon cancer, stage two. Then it was found cancer had spread to his liver. Oakes has had multiple procedures over the years to be rid of cancer, and each time it has come back. It has not been an easy road.

"I threw up for days on end. I lost almost 10 lbs. in five days," Oakes said regarding chemotherapy. All his chemotherapy treatments have been quite painful.

One of the biggest issues he has faced is the ability to use his prescribed medical cannabis while in the hospital. Some hospitals have been more understanding than others.

"They ratted me out to security and explained it to the administration. The staff doesn't know what to do. They want to be compassionate but can't because the policy is so screwed up," Oakes said regarding the St. Barnabas hospital in Monmouth County, New Jersey.

"When dealing with the machine, you start to feel like meat," Oakes said.

However, the Robert Wood Johnson Hospital in New Brunswick, NJ, was more understanding.

"I had 40 percent of liver resected. Even doctors whispered in (my wife) Mary's ear to break policy rules so her husband could have his cannabis tonight," Oakes said. "And I commend those doctors till the cows come home. Because they went with their morals, that touched me profoundly."

"Doctors there were supportive. It saved my life at that point," Oakes said regarding medical marijuana use in a hospital. "It's very difficult to navigate. A lot of patients get in trouble with the law due to minor things that hit them."

What is most notable about him is that he has not sunk into despair due to his cancer. On the contrary, he said that "I saw my cancer was an opportunity."

Oakes noted that the patients who do not openly discuss their condition and get exceedingly depressed are the ones who don't live especially long after their diagnosis.

"Jeff always says he feels like he got this for a reason," his wife Mary said.

Even while he is sick, he, along with Sativa Cross, plans to push for the legalization of cannabis in the November ballot referendum with a new organization called #Vote Cannabis 2020 that will focus on grassroots efforts to get the vote out in its favor, especially among patients.

When first prescribed with cannabis as a treatment, Oakes said people he knew were not receptive to his use. When he went to the town council meeting in his hometown of Oceanport to speak in favor of expanding the medical marijuana program, they told him to take his concerns to Trenton. Oakes later went to a Berkeley Township council meeting to speak in favor of medical marijuana and met Edward "Lefty" Grimes. They became close quickly. Oakes has since been quite active with Lefty's activist group and podcast Sativa Cross going to town council meetings and urging them to support the establishment of a medical dispensary in town. Being an activist has given him zest.

"I'm happy to have them in my life," Oakes said. He lamented that due to his illness, he has not been able to participate in their weekly podcast. Lefty spoke well of him at a homegrow rally in November 2019 when addressing the crowd.

One victory Oakes is happy about is that the Monmouth County racetrack became handicap accessible at their request and allows patients to medicate on their premises.

"They just said to use the designated smoking area," Oakes said.

Oakes cited the Jake Honig Act as a particularly good victory since it enabled the NJ MMJ program to grow exponentially.

"Jake's law was wonderful," Oakes said. "To see that law signed into effect was a nice lift for everybody.

Unfortunately, Oakes and Sativa Cross have lost more often than they have won.

"We're poo-pooed as stoners, yet we're advocating for cops to get their cards and for kids with brain tumors," Oakes said.

Oakes' activism has been praised by Scott Rudder, the President of the New Jersey Cannabis Business Association. Rudders wrote in an association email that "The road to ending cannabis prohibition has been long and painful for many. There are countless heroes who've dedicated their life, their freedom and their health, to changing the hearts and minds of lawmakers and community leaders. Jeff Oakes is one of them...He and many others like him, those who have suffered through health or an injustice, remind us all of what legalization is all about."

CHAPTER 7

THE MEDICAL MARIJUANA INDUSTRY

Slowly but surely, medical dispensaries are opening around the country as medical marijuana becomes legal. The Multi-State Operator (MSO) Green Thumb Industries (GTI) opened as the seventh medical marijuana dispensary in New Jersey under the name "Rise Dispensaries" in December 2019. GTI sold cannabis flower grown and sold by Curaleaf in Bellmawr, New Jersey. GTI planted their first crop of plants shortly before opening in mid-December 2019. The seed to sale process generally takes three months.

GTI portrays themselves as equitably minded, claiming 90 percent of their staff is from Paterson, NJ, which is known to be a city in which a majority of the citizens are racial minorities. Many companies in the cannabis industry have been criticized for being predominately made up of white men who are getting wealthy, like most other industries.

The operation is run by Devra Karlebach, CEO of GTI New Jersey. GTI is a publicly-traded MSO that holds licenses and operates dispensaries across the country. The Paterson dispensary was their 37th store in the country. In 2018, there was a lottery in New Jersey for six licenses, and GTI was one of the winners. It was the only cannabis dispensary that had opened a location by December 2019.

Paterson exemplifies a city that would benefit from a cannabis dispensary and the "Green Rush." Having been one of the first sites of industrialization in the United States, economic development in

Paterson declined for years, which exacerbated crime, depopulation, and blight. It is a city that needs help. Paterson Mayor Andre Sayegh has been in favor of cannabis reform and a dispensary coming to his city.

"We are incredibly encouraged by the investment GTI has made in Paterson and their commitment to hire Patersonians," Sayegh said. "We believe this is just the tip of the iceberg for jobs and financial benefits for our residents connected to the medical cannabis industry."

In February 2020, the New Jersey Department of Health (NJDOH) announced that MPX had been approved to start growing cannabis at their facility in Pleasantville, New Jersey, across the bay from Atlantic City. Melting Pot Extracts (MPX) is owned by iAnthus Holding Company, Inc. The cultivation facility has 33,000 square feet and includes an extraction lab and a kitchen to produce edibles.

According to Chief Strategy Officer and Director at iAnthus, Beth Stavola, the dispensary was initially going to be opened in early March 2020, before the Coronavirus pandemic spread. The dispensary will be in Atlantic City at 1575 South New York Avenue. It is called "Be," as in "Be healthy" or "Be your best self." As CEO of MPX, Stavola won the license to build an Alternative Treatment Care (ATC) facility in Atlantic City in 2018, before iAnthus bought it. MPX was one of the six companies that won a medical license in 2018.

Stavola looked across the state for suitable properties. There seemed to be an opportunity in Atlantic City, and she took it. Hopefully, it will help Atlantic City. That city needs it. Stavola said the situation reminds her of Las Vegas, where the owner of Zappos, a shoe company, invested millions in reviving the downtown area.

"It's totally awesome now," she said regarding downtown Vegas after it was initially very dilapidated. She noted she is worked with developer Pat Fasano who redeveloped Asbury Park, NJ. He is now looking to revitalize Atlantic City by building a new hotel, bars, and restaurants. After working elsewhere in the country, she is happy to be opening a dispensary in New Jersey.

"We are thrilled to be entering the New Jersey market, my home state, and our milestone tenth state market," Stavola said. "We greatly look forward to servicing the medical marijuana community and being part of a path forward toward full adult-legalization."

It has been quite a journey for Stavola and MPX. Stavola built MPX into an MSO in its own right before the company was purchased. At the time, they were operating in Nevada, California, Massachusetts, and Arizona. She initially had a successful career on Wall Street, from which she retired to focus on raising her six children. While officially retired, she was making personal investments when a broker approached her, asking if she was interested in investing $1 million in a clinical cannabis dispensary based in Arizona.

"I said no 100 times before I said yes," Stavola said. After getting over her initial hesitation, she took the plunge. But it has not been easy.

"Everything is hard in marijuana, a lot of blood, sweat, and tears. A lot of money I never knew I was going to get back," Stavola said. She added there was also a great stigma about the industry in New Jersey at the time. It was exacerbated by former Governor Chris Christie's exceedingly negative attitude toward it. However, time and a new Governor have changed the climate.

Having built up MPX, Stavola sold it to iAnthus. She remains CEO of MPX and has joined iAnthus as their Chief Strategy Officer. iAnthus owns and operates licensed cannabis cultivation, processing, and dispensary facilities across the country. Combined with MPX, they have 42 dispensary licenses across the country, including stores in which they have minority ownership and those that have yet to be opened. Stavola said that iAnthus was the right fit for MPX in part because it was operating in states they were not.

"They are absolutely terrific, great business partners," Stavola said. "It's great."

Because she has won many licenses and built a successful company,

Stavola is respected in the industry and speaks at many events.

The ninth medical marijuana dispensary opened to the public in New Jersey in February 2020 as "The Botanist," on the Atlantic City boardwalk.[100] It was initially supposed to open June 2019. Nonetheless, they opened ahead of MPX. They had hoped to prevent the opening of "Be" but failed.

The Botanist is run by the Compassionate Care Foundation (CCF). It is a satellite of their prime location in nearby Egg Harbor. That location charges $472 an ounce for cannabis flower, which is said to be in the middle of the price range for New Jersey dispensaries.

Atlantic City's leaders hope medical marijuana will prove to be a source of economic growth for the beleaguered city.

"We're also interested in adding to the excitement of revamping Atlantic City and being a part of the economic growth of the city, and providing employment and economic opportunity," said CCF Board Chairman Dave Knowlton.

"It's been a long trek to get this done," said Knowlton. The Botanist's official address is 1301 Boardwalk, which was previously a restaurant. For the first month, the Botanist only offered flower products for sale. It was unfortunate because many patients would have benefited more from other products. However, the NJ Department of Health (DOH) allowed them to sell oil in a syringe after about a month.

"This is another step forward in increasing access to medicinal marijuana for patients," said NJDOH Commissioner Judith Persichilli.

If New Jersey approves the adult-use cannabis legalization referendum in November 2020, the Botanist will be able to sell adult-use cannabis as well due to a grandfathering clause.

Once a medical marijuana program is established, doctors are needed to prescribe it to patients. One of the more prominent companies doing so is Canna Care Docs, a chain of doctor's offices specializing in prescribing medical marijuana to patients. They opened their fifth New Jersey location in Woodbury in February 2020, having decided that proximity to the Curaleaf ATC in Bellmawr would make it convenient for patients to visit after an appointment with them.

The city of Woodbury welcomed them. The Mayor and members of the City Council participated in the ribbon-cutting because they saw it as helpful to the area's redevelopment.

"Those are the best places for us to be. We're bringing a brand-new industry to an area that needs that economic stimulus. Patients are going next door to get coffee or Charlie Brown's while they wait," said Erica Pukatsch, Canna Care Docs' Regional Manager for New Jersey, Delaware, and Pennsylvania. "Being friends with our neighbors is going to allow our patients to live stigma-free as well."

Since the list of qualifying conditions was expanded in New Jersey, it has become easier for patients seeking relief; at the same time, the stigma around medical marijuana is disappearing. When Pukatsch started working in medical cannabis six years ago in Delaware, few doctors participated in the medical marijuana program. To spread awareness, the company has worked with nonprofit programs, providing discount certificates, referral programs, and veteran-centered events.

Canna Care Docs took over operations of New Jersey Alternative Medicine (NJAM) on July 1, 2019. Their other New Jersey offices are in Princeton, Morristown, Nutley, and Linwood. Kevin Kafka started the company in Massachusetts in 2012. He later sold Canna Care Docs to the company that became CB 2 Insights. Canna Care Docs operates 34 clinics in 17 states across the country. Thus, they are one of the largest chains of prescribing doctor's offices in the country. The company also operates in Canada, the United Kingdom, and Colombia.

Many patients of Canna Care Docs are professionals, doctors, and leaders in their communities. Those who are older are more likely to have the strongest prohibitionist attitudes. However, due to pain and conditions from aging, they often benefit the most.

"Educating patients about cannabis is life-changing. It's the opportunity between getting so-so relief out of the medicine or maybe having a bad experience with it and not getting relief versus completely 180 changing their life," said Ellys Thynne, Cannabis Educator at Canna Care Docs. "I've seen patients go from not walking to they're able to walk. Patients who weren't able to work and they started a business."

Thynne said that some of the basic advice she gives patients is "Experiment, try different strains, try different methods, try different doses. Start low and go slow. So, keep track, take notes."

She said they need to make sure the strains patients consume help with their issues and allow people to be the best they can be. Thynne added some patients are afraid of getting high from cannabis. They are unaware there are strains of cannabis with low doses of THC that help with the pain. Also, topicals can ease inflammations without side effects. Many patients never knew using medical marijuana to treat their condition was an option.

Thynne explained that the popular dichotomy of cannabis strains being either Sativa or Indica is outdated. Cannabis would be better classified by cannabinoid and terpene profiles.

"Sativa gives you a head high. Indica gives you a body high. (But) you can only be high in your head," Thynne said. "Any strain could do one of those things. All strains are hybrids. They've all been crossbred...over tens of thousands of years coming together."

When describing the state of being high from cannabis, most people end up describing something akin to what experts have classified as a "head high" or a "body high." A head high feels more cerebral and usually more euphoric. When you feel a body high, you are more prone to being awed by special effects in a movie and not chatty. [101] But to Thynne's point, in both cases, the THC in cannabis is making it to receptors in the brain, which then affects how you feel.

CHAPTER 8

LEGALIZATION STATE BY STATE

E ach state has had its own journey to legalization. Laws permitting different cannabis businesses vary state by state. States that legalized clinical cannabis via referendums have seen the need to pass legislation to refine their cannabis markets. The more states that legalize, the more it looks like a good idea for the others.

Erik Altieri is the Executive Director of the National Organization for the Reform of Marijuana Laws (NORML). He has seen great changes in cannabis policy since he started in the field.

"When I started on this, we had zero adult-use states, about a dozen medical marijuana states. Public opinion changes, and its trajectory gives me hope. Everything has moved the way we wanted to move," Altieri said.

When Altieri started working on legalization during the George W. Bush administration, he said the best NORML could do was provide legal advice and keep their heads down. In 2000 there was 35 percent support for cannabis legalization in the United States. As of July 2020, 67 percent of Americans support legalization, according to Altieri. Thus, while some might see the long arc of prohibition and lament how long it is taking to end, Altieri said it was encouraging that cannabis policy has changed so much in the last 15 years.

"We won the policy battle and public opinion," Altieri said. He added that medical marijuana polls at 92 percent approval. "That makes it as popular as grandma's apple pie."

Altieri said medical marijuana exposed folks who would not have otherwise been exposed to it see the relief it gave people from cancer treatments, among other conditions.

The two factors to which he credits the shift in public opinion are the developments in technology and demographic changes. Social media makes information easier to obtain for the general public and allows NORML to bypass editorial boards and corporate media, which often do not question prohibition. It is a lot easier now for people to do research, which allows them to make up their minds.

Altieri also attributed the shift in attitude to demographic change. The Greatest Generation (people who lived through the Great Depression and WWII) had limited exposure to cannabis itself and more exposure to reefer madness propaganda. Baby boomers, in the 1960s and 70s, often experienced cannabis themselves or knew someone who did. Now Millennials and Generation Z are said to support it by 85 percent plus support.

Since legalization support is now around 67 percent, giving NORML incredible political leverage. Altieri attributed this change to its high level of grassroots support, together with its D.C. office and network.

"NORML ... since our founding is a marijuana consumers lobby protecting the interests of everyday consumers, not special interest groups," Altieri said.

He explained that their broad support gives them the ability to raise a lot of money with an average donation amount of $20. They accomplish that through their chapter network. Their many volunteers and local chapters educate and empower citizens to take policy action by writing letters to legislators, calling them, hosting lobby days where people lobby legislators in person, and performing public outreach to grow the organization. Altieri said getting citizens to hound elected officials and push them to the changes they want to see is especially important.

"It might seem like they're not listening, but they log every call and what it's about, and tally how many calls. If legislators get 50, 100 calls, they notice," he said. "They work for you. They have to take your call, take your meeting. As easy as it is to be disillusioned, it does work. "We didn't get change because politicians changed; thousands of people put in the time and effort to make that happen."

"We see across the board, the nitty-gritty of organizing year after year, all building on itself. We really are on that tipping point," Altieri said. In the trajectory of all social movements, change starts state by state.

An initiative to legalize marijuana for recreational purposes was on the ballot in Michigan in November 2018.[102] It passed due to widespread support in the polls. The Michigan Regulation and Taxation of Marihuana Act now allows those who are 21 and older to purchase cannabis for recreational use legally.[103] Individuals can carry up to 2.5 ounces and have 10 ounces at their home. They can also grow up to 12 plants. Municipalities have the right to ban businesses from distributing cannabis within their respective limits. A mandatory 10 percent tax is collected on marijuana products sold in addition to the state's 6 percent sales tax. The 10 percent sales tax is lower than the tax in Colorado at 15 percent, Oregon at 17 percent, Washington at 37 percent, and California at 15 percent at a minimum.[104]

The ballot initiative in Michigan did not include reforms to the criminal justice system that would wipe away the charges of many previous offenders of marijuana-related crimes. Supporters of the initiative sought to displace the underground marijuana market in addition to raising revenue to pay for a wide variety of efforts, including $20 million to fund research to treat PTSD. Thirty-five percent of the money from the sales tax goes to funding K-12 education within the state, another 35 percent goes towards improving infrastructure, 15 percent to cities in relation to the number of cannabis businesses within their limits, and 15 percent goes to county governments using the same metric.

The driving force behind the initiative was the Coalition to Regulate Marijuana Like Alcohol. They campaigned for months to have the initiative placed on the ballot.

"While we would have been happy to see our initiative passed by the legislature as written, we are confident Michigan voters understand that marijuana prohibition has been an absolute disaster and that they will agree that taxing and regulating marijuana is a far better solution," said coalition spokesperson Josh Hovey in June 2018.

The coalition was composed of a range of pro-cannabis advocates, including the ACLU of Michigan, the Drug Policy Alliance, MI Legalize, National Patient Rights Association, the Michigan chapter of NORML, the Marijuana Law Section of the State Bar of Michigan, and the Michigan Cannabis Coalition, among others.

"Multiple polls show that roughly 60 percent of Michigan voters want to see marijuana legalized and regulated but, as we saw with the legislative debates these past few weeks, there is still a lot of misinformation out there," said Hovey. "The fact is that our proposal is carefully written to be a model for responsible cannabis regulations and closely follows the medical marijuana licensing law passed by the state legislature in 2016."

Attorney General Dana Nessel was elected in 2018 alongside the ballot referendum, which she supported. She has been a firm supporter of legalization for many years. Nessel won a close primary in April 2018 over a candidate who had a far weaker position on the issue. Nessel's campaign website stated that "Michigan needs common-sense licensing and regulation of cannabis manufacturing and distribution. When elected, I will work with the legislature and local law enforcement to ensure a safe market that keeps cannabis out of kids' hands and off the roads."

While Michigan had not elected a Democratic attorney general in 16 years, many predicted that it would be a good year for the Democrats. Gretchen Whitmer, the Democratic nominee for Governor in 2018 who also won, supported legalization.

Healthy and Productive Michigan was the principal opponent of the initiative and had support from a law enforcement association. They ran an aggressive ad campaign across radio, TV, and Facebook. Medical marijuana had been legal for ten years before the ballot campaign. Michigan was the tenth state to legalize adult-use cannabis.

In Colorado, Governor Jared Polis signed a series of marijuana bills into law in May 2019 that was expected to greatly revamp the state's cannabis market by allowing cannabis to be consumed at social lounges and permitting marijuana home delivery.[105]

"Up until this bill, there's been no way to have safe public consumption. I've smelled it walking my dog. For many of us with kids, we want to make sure we don't have that in our neighborhoods," Polis said. A third bill signed by Polis allows publicly traded companies to own marijuana-based companies. Polis became Governor of Colorado in early 2019. He was previously a Member of the House of Representatives and a long-time champion of cannabis legalization. Governor Polis played an instrumental role in the growth of the state's medical and recreational marijuana markets by campaigning for their passage.

House Bill 1230 paved the way for social cannabis consumption in Colorado, providing for the first-time public spaces where consumption is permitted. Tasting room licenses allow marijuana businesses to sell marijuana and marijuana-related products while also serving as a lounge where customers can use their cannabis recreationally. Licenses for hospitality spaces will allow businesses to serve as a legal place for people to bring their cannabis for consumption. The implementation of hospitality spaces will depend on local governments. Under Colorado's cannabis law, cities can form their policies around the regulation of cannabis and have the option to prohibit sales and consumption sites.

House Bill 1234 allowed for home delivery of cannabis for both medical and adult-use marijuana consumers. Under the new law, medical marijuana can be delivered to individual homes beginning in January 2020, while recreational marijuana operations must wait a year before beginning to do so. In Colorado, customers must be at least 18 years old and registered with the state's medical cannabis program to purchase medical marijuana, and at least 21 to purchase recreational marijuana.

For patients who have difficulty traveling, receiving their medication at home will be helpful. However, not everyone can partake in the cannabis delivery service. The law excludes deliveries to college dorms. In California, home delivery was legal before it was in Colorado. Companies in California have been able to successfully lure drivers away from Uber and Lyft with the promise of providing health benefits.

Another bill Polis signed was House Bill 1090, which allowed publicly traded companies and outside investment into the state's cannabis industry. Colorado had previously banned publicly traded companies from participating in the market. The law was expected to introduce new cannabis products to Colorado from companies that had been unable to operate in the state. Colorado was one of the first states to adopt recreational cannabis and had a thriving industry as a result. The state hit a new monthly sales record in March 2019, generating more than $112 million.

Polis also signed into law bills that gave medical marijuana access to patients diagnosed with autism and, as an alternative to painkillers. Colorado's previous governor, John Hickenlooper (D), only reluctantly supported cannabis reform at times. He vetoed a similar marijuana hospitality bill while Governor.

In 2019, Illinois became the 11th state to legalize adult-use cannabis. January 1, 2020 was the first day consumers could purchase and consume adult-use cannabis legally in the state. Illinois Lt. Governor Juliana Stratton (D) was one of the first customers to purchase cannabis at the Sunnyside Lakeview dispensary in Chicago. It was the first time a Lt. Governor publicly purchased cannabis. Passage of cannabis reform was a priority of Illinois Governor J.B. Pritzker (D) when he first took office in January 2019, having been elected in the 2018 midterm elections. He signed legalization into law in June 2019. But it was decided legalization would not take effect until New Year's Day 2020.

Renzo Mejia of Chicago made the first legal purchase in Illinois when he bought an eighth of an ounce for $80 at a Chicago dispensary.[106] Mejia is a patient in the Illinois medical marijuana (or clinical cannabis) program and has worked in the industry as well.

Many thought the prices were higher than that of cannabis obtained via the underground market. Part of the reason the price is high is due to the level of taxation imposed on cannabis. Illinois officials are eager for the state to reap the benefit of a brand-new stream of tax revenue to fill budget gaps. California has been dealing with similar issues. Now that prohibition is over in Illinois, people can be open about their use and support for cannabis, which should further build support for legalization.

"It always should have been legalized," said Police Officer Jeremy Eaton of Joliet, IL. "We need to break that stigma about police and cannabis, and I want to let people know that we're not the bad guy."

No criminal incidents were reported, while many waited in the cold to buy cannabis on the first day of the recreational market. On the contrary, the people waiting in line were described as jovial gatherings with cars honking their horns in support as they drove by at some locations. Dispensary lines were long on the first day. Some people had been lining up since the previous night to buy cannabis. One dispensary offered those waiting in line hot chocolate, coffee, and a warm tent to wait in.

Customers appreciated the convenience and legality of the dispensaries' cannabis. Legal cannabis is thought to be safer than its illegal counterpart. Common issues such as limited purchase options and shortages of products were reported at some dispensaries. One individual tried to buy flower at two dispensaries before finding one that had not sold out. Technical issues with the state tracking system that monitored cannabis sales also caused delays. Most of the open dispensaries in Illinois were previously exclusively medical dispensaries that kept products for patients in reserve despite the great demand for adult-use cannabis.

Individuals from other states visited Illinois with the sole purpose of buying legal cannabis. While it is legal to do so, it remains illegal to take legal cannabis across state lines. It is a holdover from federal prohibition that remains even if you are traveling between two legal states.

Social justice advocates, meanwhile, who sought to eradicate fallout from the War on Drugs, got their wish. Governor Pritzker began the process of pardoning 11,017 individuals convicted of small amounts of cannabis possession up to 30 grams on December 31, 2019.

"Illinois is putting equity first, clearing thousands of convictions and giving individuals and their families a new lease on life," Pritzker declared regarding the pardons.[107] One of the criticisms of the states that legalized cannabis early was the lack of social equity provisions built into their laws.

"Illinois is going where no other state has before, admitting the unjust errors of the war on drugs and giving so many Illinoisans greater opportunities to build good lives for themselves and the people they love," Stratton said. She added that thousands more would be pardoned shortly. Illinois sought to include social justice provisions in its legalization bill to address the evil of the drug war.

"Our Restore, Reinvest and Renew program will direct 25 percent of the state's cannabis revenue right back into the communities hit the hardest by decades of over-policing, disinvestment, disenfranchisement, and violence," Stratton added. "In that effort, we're lifting up the voices of the people who actually live in these neighborhoods, who know these blocks and exactly where our dollars will make a real difference."

Not every fight in legalization has been won. On the contrary, many cannabis advocates know defeat all too well. New Jersey is the best example of this since efforts to pass cannabis reform failed twice in 2019. Advocates have been pushing hard for legalization since Governor Phil Murphy (D) was first elected in 2017.

"We were all excited when Governor Murphy got in, that the state would see legalization happen rapidly. Unfortunately, it wasn't that simple, but we have made significant progress," said Tara "Misu" Sargente, Executive Director of the New Jersey Cannabis Business Association (NJCBA).

Murphy was unable to horse trade or otherwise sway Senators Ron Rice (D-Essex) and Dick Codey (D-Essex), an ardent supporter of his gubernatorial campaign. Rice is a former police officer, while Codey was swayed by old propaganda. Legislators have been inundated by the efforts of lobbyists representing pharmaceutical companies, who likely fear cannabis cutting into their profit margins, and religious interests to block legalization. Rehabilitation centers also fear a cut into their profits and have been boosting the opposition. In spring 2019, it was announced that the failed comprehensive cannabis reform bill would be broken into separate parts and passed in that fashion. The Jake Honig Act, for example, expanded New Jersey's paltry medical marijuana program was originally part of the comprehensive reform bill.

In November 2019, after the State Assembly elections, proponents thought it might be possible to pass cannabis reform in the lame-duck session, the time between the election and the beginning of the new session. Thus, shortly after the election, New Jersey legislators and cannabis advocates held a press conference in Trenton to announce the "94 No More" campaign to legalize adult-use cannabis.

Among the cannabis advocates assembled were the ACLU & New Jersey United for Marijuana Reform (NJUMR), the Coalition for Medical Marijuana in New Jersey (CMMNJ), the NJCBA, Garden State NORML, the New Jersey Cannabis Industry Association (NJCIA), the United Farm and Commercial Workers (UFCW), the Teamsters union, the NJ NAACP, and Doctors for Cannabis Regulation (DFCR), along with a few lobbyists.

"I echo Michelle Alexander, that this is a new era of Jim Crow," said Reverend Stephen Green, a pastor based in Roselle, regarding the high amount of arrests in the state. "With the Red Sea before us, we cannot relent and wait another year."

He also called for automatic expungement, diversity of business owners to be encouraged, and for tax dollars from legal cannabis to be reinvested in the communities most devastated by the War on Drugs. According to the ACLU, more than 34,500 individuals are being arrested each year in New Jersey, which averages 94 a day. Every year, the arrest statistics for cannabis possession worsen.

Senator Nick Scutari (D-Union), who introduced the legalization bill S. 2703 into the Senate, noted that he first introduced a cannabis reform a decade ago, and many laughed at it. He too, lamented the arrest statistics.

"It feels like law enforcement is saying 'let's get as many as we can get now," Scutari said, referring to the statistics. "The time is now for action." He added that 65 percent of New Jersey favors cannabis reform.

"We're close," Scutari said. "We're closer than we've ever been before." He added that the statistics would only get worse unless reform is passed. Being arrested for possession and a subsequent felony can negatively affect one's ability to go to college, get a good-paying job, and even enter the military. It costs New Jersey about $140 million to arrest individuals for possession and process them. Assemblyman Jamal Holley (D-Union) pointed out that the statistics collected on arrests are used by law enforcement to secure more funding.

"People that look like me are targeted every single day," said Holley, the primary sponsor of the bill in that chamber.

"We have the votes in the Assembly," Holley assured the audience. It echoed similar confidence felt by other sources regarding the Assembly.[108] Holley later explained that a bill passed by the legislature was preferable to a referendum because it could be more comprehensive. Before the press conference, an advocate mentioned that legislators had said there was an insufficient amount of grassroots efforts to let legislators know that their constituents were in favor of it. That was not the first time that sentiment was voiced.

However, a couple of hours after that press conference, it was announced by State President Steve Sweeney (D-Gloucester) and Scutari that the adult-use cannabis legalization bill was dead.[109] Instead, there would be a referendum in 2020, setting reform and its implementation back by at least a year, if not two. It was said that Sweeney only needed a few more votes for the bill to pass the Senate. Thus, despite the enthusiasm for the new lame-duck session push for reform, the effort was in vain.

Leo Bridgewater, among others, was not happy about the news that a ballot referendum will decide on new Jersey's cannabis legalization.

"We're screwed," he said regarding the referendum. "Historically, any states that have legalized cannabis through ballot referendum wish they hadn't. Every contingency that New Jersey has sent to Vegas, Colorado, or California all warned don't do this by referendum."

Bridgewater explained that the state seemed to be planning on taking the entire industry with all its nuances and oversimplifying to a "yes or no" question, to the detriment of those fighting for the inclusion of criminal justice and small business assistance provisions. The opposition of legalization from State Senators Rice and Shirley Turner

(D-Mercer), prominent African American leaders in Trenton, likely exacerbated the problem.

"They're the Flintstones to my Jetsons," Bridgewater said. In his opinion, their stubbornness is astounding, given the industry's potential to help inner-city communities. The problem with politicians that represent communities of color staunchly opposing legalizations means that legalization may not contain provisions that benefit their constituents. Without these important voices, Bridgewater feels it is much harder for cannabis activists to secure key criminal justice and small business provisions included in the final legislation.

The vast amount of economic opportunities opened by cannabis reform include good, white-collar jobs and potential businesses such as one that uses hemp in the construction of urban communities.

"We're rebuilding the hood," Bridgewater said, adding that local cannabis-based businesses can benefit each other and their community.

"New Jersey could be number two in (tax) revenue after California," Bridgewater said. "At what point do you start talking about that money?"

It was noted that the vast majority of cannabis C-suite executives are middle-aged or older white men.

"So historically, this industry hasn't been kind to people of color and women, and one of the ways it has gotten so bad is ballot referendums," he explained. "This presents a disaster for us."

The fact that a referendum was decided as the best course of action was illuminating to him.

"That tells me as an African American man in New Jersey, the big business of locking us up is something that's a regular thing here and when you do a ballot referendum, even when warned not to, and it is New Jersey, the fix is in."

Pointing to Big Pharma, the alcohol industry fearing competition, and the Prison-Industrial Complex, Bridgewater said that was the reason reform was halted. But a referendum does offer hope of victory at a later date. So, it was not a total loss for cannabis advocates.

"I'll certainly support it and urge others to support it," said Ken Wolski, Executive Director of the CMMNJ, regarding the referendum. "But it just kicks the can down the road another year. It's disappointing for me and for the marijuana reform advocates of New Jersey."

Wolski was realistic about the difficulty of passing cannabis reform, saying, "There was never tremendous support for it. I was surprised they were going to take it up in lame duck."

CMMNJ, along with Garden State NORML, the NJCBA, and DFCR, made a video to promote reform during the lame-duck session.[110] Wolski lamented that the effort to legalize cannabis in the lame-duck session was so brief, he was not able to send it to the legislators. However, he was stoic about the effort saying, "We're no strangers to being disappointed. Some of us have been at this for a very long time."

"I always have doubts with politicians," Assemblyman Holley said when asked about his optimism regarding its passage at the initial press conference. It turns out that line was more than just a throwaway joke since the failure of the "94 no more" effort occurred mere hours later. "Ninety-four no more" is a reference to the number of arrests in the state per day from a study done by the ACLU.

There was great speculation that political tensions over corporate tax reform, among other issues, between the exceedingly moderate State Senate President, a union leader, and the more progressive Governor Phil Murphy, a wealthy banker, impeded cannabis reform. These tensions erupted into full view in November 2019 on the same day as the "94 No More" press conference. Sue Altman, the Executive Director of New Jersey Working Families, a staunch ally of the Governor, was forcibly dragged from a committee room. At the same time, George E. Norcross III, the undisputed boss of South Jersey, grinned as he watched.[111] Norcross and Sweeney are old friends. Some cynics said the South Jersey Democrats did not want to give

Murphy, who campaigned for the Governorship on legalization, a "win."

It is believed that cannabis reform would pass on the ballot by a great margin, especially in a presidential election year. While ballot referendums are not common in New Jersey, compared to California, where the process is easier for people to utilize, positive referendums have passed. For example, in 2013, despite Chris Christie winning election as Governor, a referendum to raise the minimum wage passed. But ballot questions in New Jersey usually seem esoteric, poorly worded, and receive little media attention. The ballot question in New Jersey will say:

"Do you approve amending the Constitution to legalize a controlled form of marijuana called 'cannabis'? Only adults at least 21 years of age could use cannabis. The State commission created to oversee the State's medical cannabis program would also oversee the new, personal use cannabis market. Cannabis products would be subject to the State sales tax. If authorized by the Legislature, a municipality may pass a local ordinance to charge a local tax on cannabis products."

"We support any move beyond prohibition," said Charlana McKeithen, Executive Director of Garden State NORML about the referendum. "Now, marijuana consumers and anyone who supports reform can cast a vote for freedom."[112]

Tara "Misu" Sargente was optimistic about the referendum.

"I have faith in my state," she added. "November will be here before we know it. There's light at the end of the tunnel. There's a timeline. I've waited a decade. What's a year?"

In addition to the expansion of the state's medical marijuana program, another bill that passed in New Jersey in 2019 expunged the criminal records of those with past cannabis convictions. However, while cannabis is still illegal in New Jersey, more people will likely be convicted and need their records expunged once the adult-use of cannabis is legalized. Thus, it became a piecemeal measure stemming from the failure of the legislature to pass a comprehensive cannabis bill in the spring.

"It's easy to get defeated. But I practice gratitude. I believe in what we're doing. If you look at the small stuff, we're making progress," Misu said.

CHAPTER 9

HOMEGROW

The ability to grow cannabis at home, known as homegrow, is a controversial issue. In many states, the cannabis being sold at dispensaries is going for high. What is worse, the cannabis sold is not always top-shelf quality. Certain strains are only available at certain times. It becomes exceedingly difficult if you are relying on a specific cannabis strain as a daily medication, as many patients do.

Thus, if patients could merely grow cannabis, they would not be burdened by its extremely high price. Because it is not covered by health insurance, patients are often forced to pay $300 or more for an ounce of the cannabis they desperately need.

The Multi-State Operators (MSOs) often oppose homegrow because they feel it would cut into their sales. In fact, in New York, they sent a letter to Governor Andrew Cuomo, decrying its supposedly negative effects on their business.[113] Among the signers of the letter were the MSOs MedMen, Columbia Care, PharmaCann, the Botanist, Acreage NY, Etain, and Vireo Health. The effort was led by the New York Medical Cannabis Industry Association. NORML and the Drug Policy Alliance (DPA) criticized the letter. After public outrage, some of the companies tried to backpedal on it. Washington State is the only legalized state without homegrow.

Homegrow is an especially contentious issue in New Jersey. Long-time advocates and new activists gathered in the state capital of Trenton in November 2019 to rally for cannabis legalization and homegrow for medical marijuana patients. Homegrow is especially popular and a rallying point for many New Jersey activists. It would benefit patients, who due to their illness, cannot work a great deal and struggle to pay for expensive medical marijuana on a lean budget. Because patients fear arrest, they do not want to grow it illegally, which itself is relatively easy. However, the crime is treated as more severe than simple possession. In addition to the price, advocates decry the poor quality of cannabis from the medical dispensaries in the state.

"If I have to march every couple weeks, then you'll see me," said Derylyn Jones, "DJ" Stokes, to the crowd regarding the need to fight persistently for change. Among those gathered were Ken Wolski of CMMNJ, CMMNJ Board Member Jim Miller, Edward "Lefty" Grimes, leading activist and host of the Sativa Cross Ignorance is No Excuse podcast, and the prominent radical activist Ed "NJWeedman" Forchion. DJ Stokes and Sanjay Chaudhari organized the protest with support from the activists mentioned above.

"This isn't just me saying this. There's 200, 300 people involved in this. We have a louder voice," said Chaudhari regarding the value of rallying activists. He added that he felt homegrow was a reasonable demand. Chaudhari is a patient himself and experienced in growing other plants. Homegrow is an issue many Trenton insiders do not think has a good chance of passage through the legislature, despite the grassroots demand and its inclusion in legalization elsewhere in the country.

"Legalization, not corporatization!" the crowd chanted multiple times. A variety of pro-cannabis activists joined Lefty's podcast, including Brian Powers, a long-time radical activist and host of "#NJRR Live" on New Jersey Revolution Radio. He said thousands of activists are needed to flood the Statehouse and smoke inside it to demand homegrow, the cessation of patients' arrests, and certain other concessions.

"If advocates seek to persuade legislators via conventional means,

"You're just kissing their ass for favors," he said.

"I want to storm that statehouse armed with pounds of weed, smoke, and go tell themselves to fuck themselves!" Powers said to the applause of the crowd, citing the examples of the labor movement and Martin Luther King's successful fight for change through civil disobedience. Wolski argued that it is more logical to fight for homegrow than fighting the corporate issues. But many disagreed with him.

"Corporate cannabis is going to ruin everything," declared one activist, believing that the product and customers would both suffer if Big Pharma entered the market. He added that in Colorado, big conglomerates have begun to control the industry to the detriment of small businesses, and those seeking strains corporations do not sell. The issues they describe are the issues that come with the nature of the current economic system. Someone summed up the situation with the blockage of adult-use cannabis as "four assholes ruining it for millions."

"A minority is strangling the majority," said another activist. The rally was planned before the defeat of cannabis reform in the legislature earlier in November 2019.

Some strident activists feel the referendum will implement the language of the failed reform bill, S. 2703, which they did not support because they did not find the bill was sufficiently inclusive nor progressive regarding criminal justice. It was also bereft of homegrow.

Regarding the hot topic of homegrow, veteran activist and cannabis businessman Leo Bridgewater said, "I think that could be a thing. Let's do this smart." He explained that he believes health caretakers should register and then be allowed to grow up to 50 plants for 20 patients. To him, registering individuals is key to the program. "There should be oversight and a smart way to do it."

Bridgewater believes that would be a way to allow legacy growers to enter the market and use their experience. "They're the ones we need the most, the ones doing it underground, in the shadows," he said.

Cannabis reform has come a long way due to diehard activists. Jim Miller has been a pillar of cannabis reform activism in New Jersey for years. He began pushing for medical marijuana reform and homegrow five years before medical marijuana reform passed in California.

Miller was in favor of cannabis reform when there were few willing to take that position. He became an activist in 1991 due to the illness of his late wife, Cheryl, who had a severe case of Multiple Sclerosis (MS). In 1993, when Miller could not convince reporters to see Cheryl consume her infused butter, and not knowing other advocates, they resolved to take drastic action. He walked across the state, pushing her wheelchair.

"I walked across the state in 1993 from Seaside to that golden dome," Miller said, referring to the New Jersey Statehouse in Trenton on the other side of the state from Seaside Heights, NJ, where they started. Miller explained that it was a 58-mile journey they completed in 25 hours.

"I had no cell phone or anything. Just a sign stating, 'Medical Marijuana for MS,'" Miller said. The walk was successful in generating press. The *Asbury Park Press* initially covered it along with some local newspapers. That led to Channel 6 ABC News, as well as the now-defunct Channel 9 UPN, both reporting on their progress. Despite her illness, Cheryl was always up for radical action.

"What are they going to do to me?" she said. Once, they went to Washington, DC, and stopped in front of Congressman Bob Barr's (R-GA) office door and refused to move.[114] Barr had made a public display of blocking funds for Washington, DC's medical marijuana program, after the city passed a ballot measure approving it. When Miller was arrested for civil disobedience, it became a news sensation.

"I'm good at slash and burn," Miller noted. After a while, he began to convince policymakers about the need for reform. He spent a great deal of time in Washington seeking meetings to persuade Members of Congress.

"And Rob Andrews was the only one who said ok. We went to an appointment in his New Jersey Office. After about a minute, Andrews stopped me and said, 'You know when I have somebody expressing their point of view like you, I usually look at it what they want to gain. And the only thing I see Cheryl has to gain is her health," Miller recounted.

Miller said Andrews was one of the first Congressmen to change his position on medical marijuana, which showed other members they could change their minds as well. They also convinced Andrews' then-Chief of Staff, Bill Caruso, who is a leader of the New Jersey United for Marijuana Reform (NJUMR) coalition. Former Congressman Rob Andrews (D-NJ) represented South Jersey from 1990 to 2014.

Unfortunately, after many years of activism and struggle, Cheryl passed away on June 7, 2003, in her husband's arms.

"It was actually kind of beautiful. It was an easy passing, no pain being expressed, just the two of us," Miller said.

In November 2003, he was a co-founder of CMMNJ with Wolski. They wanted to branch out from NORML to form a group that made patient care its central cause. Since its founding, CMMNJ has been a key group pushing for change in cannabis laws. His strident militancy stands in stark contrast to Wolski's quiet leadership.

By 2009, when the Compassionate Use of Medical Marijuana (CUMMA) Act was being debated, it looked like homegrow would become law as part of the bill establishing New Jersey's medical marijuana program. CUMMA passed the State Senate 22-16.

"All other states that had medical marijuana programs at the time also had homegrow. So, it seemed natural," Miller said. However, according to Miller, on June 4, 2009, Health Committee Chair Assemblyman Herb Conaway (D-Burlington) blindsided many when he announced changes to the bill, including the elimination of homegrow and a 10-minute discussion before voting on it would commence.

"I could feel my blood running. Everybody was numb. And it was over in short order," Miller said. He noted that former Assemblymen Michael Patrick Carroll (R-Morris), Reed Gusciora (D-Mercer), along with Senator Nick Scutari (D-Union), looked astonished. He added that they had to accept the bill as it was.

"Here we are ten years later, 13 of those 22 are still in office and haven't said boo. Its well-known patients cannot afford it," Miller said. He also explained that a significant number of patients in the program die every year because they cannot afford the cannabis sold at dispensaries. He speculated that perhaps then-Governor Jon Corzine was against homegrow. The reason homegrow was taken out of the bill was never publicly explained. Many have said in general that homegrow would be hard to regulate and could lead some to sell cannabis on the black market.

Nonetheless, after years of struggle, New Jersey's medical marijuana program is doing better than ever, and Miller remains active as a leader in the movement. And despite the hardship of fighting for so long and New Jersey's slow progress on the issue, Miller is not disheartened.

"When I go to a dispensary, I see it through Cheryl's eyes. For everybody's complaints, they don't know what's it like," Miller said. "I see people smiling when they leave. I notice every time they seem comforted by the little white bag they're holding."

When passionately articulating the need for cannabis reform, Miller has a look in his eye, like a painting of John Brown.

The Last Moments of John Brown by Thomas Hovenden
With a small band of insurgents, Brown raided Harper's Ferry Armory
in the name of emancipation.[115] Brown was executed for the raid
shortly before the Civil War. He was lionized for his deeds by
abolitionists and civil rights leaders. To this day, Brown remains a folk
hero to many.

CHAPTER 10
THE INDUSTRY BLOOMS

Today's cannabis entrepreneurs and professionals are pioneers in a brand-new industry centered around a plant with health benefits that can no longer be ignored. Many have called it the "Green Rush," like the California Gold Rush of the 19th century.

Worldwide sales of cannabis are expected to total nearly $44.8 billion by 2024, according to the seventh edition of a report by Arcview Market Research and BDS Analytics. Entitled "State of Legal Cannabis Markets" and released in June 2019, the report evaluated the "Total Cannabinoid Market," including sales of marijuana and CBD products.[116]

In the United States, total legal cannabis spending is expected to grow at a compound annual growth rate (CAGR) of 20 percent to around $30 billion domestically in 2024. The estimates were made under the assumption that adult-use cannabis legalization would continue expanding, which will help the industry triple in size. The report also forecasted that the introduction of new products to the market, such as edibles and vape pens, will offer more consumer choices and subsequently generate new sales through dispensaries, retail stores, and eventually pharmacies.

While the U.S. leads the world in marijuana market size, the global cannabis market will be bolstered by the spread of the cannabis industry to other countries. Spending on adult-use cannabis in international markets is expected to grow at a 33 percent CAGR from

2018 to 2024 to nearly $44 billion.

Full cannabis legalization in Canada in 2018 boosted the worldwide cannabis market, with the province of Ontario leading in sales, followed by Alberta, British Columbia, and Quebec. Canada's adult-use marijuana sales are projected to grow from $113 million in the partial year of 2018 to nearly $4.8 billion by 2024.

Oh Canada

Steve DeAngelo has been called "the father of the cannabis industry" and has likely done more to change cannabis than almost anyone else alive. He founded Harborside dispensary, co-founded the Arcview Group investment firm, the National Cannabis Industry Association (NCIA) to advocate for the industry, and the Last Prisoner Project (LPP) to help those unjustly imprisoned for cannabis-related crimes.

His trademark hat and braids give DeAngelo his signature look. He explained that he admires the look of Native American leader Quanah Parker, who was the last war chief of the Comanche tribe that fought the U.S. army until it became clear there was no chance of victory. He then led his people to settle and extracted better conditions from the U.S. government than many other tribes. Parker then became a prosperous farmer and businessman. DeAngelo said Parker's hat was like the "hats I wear, but he never cut his braids. And I will never cut my braids either," he said.

He has been involved in cannabis since his teens.

"I've been a cannabis activist and entrepreneur since I encountered the plant at 13. I had a transformational experience that first time and wanted cannabis to be part of my life," DeAngelo said. "I made legalization of cannabis my mission at an early age."

He was one of the leaders of the Initiative 59 referendum campaign in 1998 to legalize medical marijuana in Washington, DC. The referendum passed by 69 percent. However, Congress blocked its implementation. DeAngelo was deflated and felt the election had been stolen. So, he uprooted and went to California.

In 2006, he was awarded a clinical cannabis license in the city of Oakland, CA. He sought to make Harborside the gold standard of a dispensary. With dispensary locations throughout California, Harborside is publicly traded on the Canadian stock exchange. He then created Steep Hill laboratory to test cannabis after having issues with other labs.

Not long after, he co-founded Arcview Group with Troy Dayton, the first cannabis investment company. DeAngelo said it is one of the top 10 Angel investor networks in the United States.

However, DeAngelo said his proudest accomplishment was standing up to the federal government when they declared war on the medical marijuana industry in 2011 and terrorized dispensaries, their landlords, and their properties. It forced about a third of California's 1800 dispensaries out of business. He called it the "last stand of the federal government," which was determined to halt cannabis reform.

"Unlike the previous 600, I decided to fight them and went to California tenant court and the federal court. The City of Oakland came to our defense, and they said it would result in a public health crisis."

"Had we not done that and stood up, it would have emboldened the federal government, they might have tried to shut that down. It was the last stand of the prohibitionists, and we won," DeAngelo said. He helped legalize adult-use cannabis in California via the ballot referendum in 2016. They previously failed to legalize cannabis in 2010.

With a few others, he founded the Last Prisoner Project, which seeks to end the imprisonment of every individual convicted of a cannabis-related crime. Its genesis came in 2017 after California had passed adult-use reform, and the industry was doing well, preparing for their adult-use market to open. DeAngelo was on a business trip to Canada to raise money for his company. He went to Toronto, where he was in a conference room with people in the cannabis industry, reviewing numbers that looked good for the industry.

"The feeling was really good," he said. Then DeAngelo received a phone call.

"It was my friend Chuck calling from a correctional facility serving four years for 14 pounds of weed... On this case, Chuck was upset. It was the middle of winter, four feet of snow on the ground, and his mother had no one to dig her out. And I walked back into the conference room feeling that despair. That room was really cheery. And I was struck by that disparity," he said.

DeAngelo said he felt he had to do something to help his friend due to a moral imperative. After barely a year of operations, they have recruited a full-time staff and launched several projects, including the prisoner to prosperity pipeline. Sponsored by the MSO Harvest, LPP developed a six-week curriculum designed to train them to be successful in the legal industry. Before COVID hit, they were getting ready to deploy the class in Oakland. Unfortunately, it was delayed.

Another of their major efforts is to increase the number of clemencies (or pardons) granted by state Governors. In the adult-use legal states, they have the authority to release all cannabis prisoners. However, they do not, in part, because there is a difficult process to approve petitions. So, LLP is working with the Governors on a program to streamline the parameters.

"What used to be simple restorative justice means life and death," DeAngelo said. He explained that in states where cannabis is legalized, prisoners are stuck in jail and cannot socially distance, use sanitizer, cannot control their food, air, or water to cope with COVID-19.

"I spent weeks trying to control everything. And my friend Chuck couldn't do anything," he said.

Thus, he takes the issue very seriously.

"I hope in the not too distant future LPP can file more litigation and help those serving life without parole," he said. DeAngelo lamented what the damage the War on Drugs has done to communities of color.

"The only reason I'm walking around today is because of the color of my skin... I would have been dead or in prison right now," he said.

DeAngelo said in the future, cannabis will be the most valuable product traded in the world.

"It brings us closer to nature, helps resolve disputes, makes us more patient and loving, and it's our best chance to save this world," he said about cannabis' power.

"Sometimes I feel like an old pioneer mountain man looking down on a valley, seeing a big bustling town that's energetic and promising. Other times I look down on that valley, and it's someplace I don't really want to be," DeAngelo said. He lamented that the industry is overly taxed and regulated, which has frustrated cannabis from reaching its full potential.

"I'm really glad of the progress we made, but we have a long distance to go," he said.

Troy Dayton is one of the leading figures in the cannabis industry. He worked with DeAngelo to build the Arcview Group into the biggest investor firm in the cannabis industry. For ten years, Dayton has run Arciew, bringing entrepreneurs and investors together. He has been striving since 1995, when he was a college student at American University, to make cannabis legal.

While a freshman in college, when he borrowed rolling papers, he was invited to a meeting about cannabis reform. Thus, he became the first volunteer of the Marijuana Policy Project (MPP). Later, he was involved in starting Students for a Sensible Drug Policy (SSDP).

"It was a whole lot more rebellious than it is today," Dayton said, recalling his early activism. "I felt like a credible rebel."

To put in context how radical cannabis legalization was in 1995, between 1979 and 1995, pro-cannabis advocates consistently lost ground during the War on Drugs. It was a year before California approved the use of medical marijuana (or clinical cannabis) via the ballot referendum. There certainly was nothing resembling a legitimate cannabis industry. Support in the mid-'90s for legalization reached about 35 percent. Today it is closer to 63 percent.

Dayton worked consistently for MPP and, by 2009, became their chief fundraiser, securing donations from wealthy individuals interested in reform. By that point, though, he realized only so much could be done through pure activism.

"In the United States, you got to find out how to make it profitable. Once you spark the engine of capitalism, you could use it for change," Dayton said. He explained that the people who were donating were often doing so as an act of civil disobedience but were also interested in investing in the burgeoning medical marijuana industry. Others had interesting business ideas.

"So Arcview was birthed out of bringing these groups together in a way that was responsible and profitable, which would also help move the needle politically," Dayton said.

The company has since funded many start-ups and smaller companies that have gone on to be worth hundreds of millions of dollars. Arcview has invested in a wide range of companies in cannabis and hemp. According to Dayton, two of the most successful companies they invested in early on were MJ Freeway and Akerna. Another company, called Tokyo Smoke, was bought by Canopy Growth for $133 million. It was initially worth $4 million. Ebu, also funded by Arcview, was sold to Canopy Growth for $400 million. To date, over 215 companies have raised money through Arcview.

There are probably companies Arcview regretted not funding, but Dayton could not remember one by name off the top of his head when asked. (MassRoots is likely one, more on them later).

For companies interested in funding, Dayton explained they could apply via the Arcview website so the company can see if they are a good fit. He said Arcview looks for companies with strong teams and a product that has the potential to serve a large market. They are especially interested in those that have achieved consistent sales.

If interested, an Arcview representative reaches out to the company to arrange a video presentation to the selection committee. If the company passes, they are featured on Arcview's platform along with 50 to 100 other companies their investors can view. Some can present at select company events. Then they are paired with mentors and advisors who introduce them to investors. The minimum investment in a company is between $50,000 and $100,000. To invest in Arcview, you must be an accredited investor who has a liquid net worth of at least $1 million or earned $200,000 annually for the last two years.

For those interested in getting into the cannabis industry, Dayton said people should figure out what they already know and apply it to the cannabis sector. Dayton also said there are tremendous opportunities for companies to develop software and logistics to assist the industry.

"There's always room for a better mousetrap," Dayton said. "There's always an opportunity to unseat any of the incumbents."

There also remains a lot of room for innovation in the sector.

"We're going to find new ways to utilize molecules of this new plant," Dayton said. In the future, Dayton sees cannabis becoming merely another consumer packaged good. He believes it will be like the wine industry where you have a few big companies but many other mom and pop brands.

As dispensaries pop up and the industry becomes larger and larger, national trade shows become important. In December 2019, 35,000 people from 75 countries gathered at the mammoth Las Vegas Convention Center for MJ Biz Con, "the premier global cannabis industry event." MJ Biz Con offers opportunities to players in all aspects of the cannabis industry. For those who have been dreaming of cannabis becoming legal and treated like any other commodity, it is a great thing to see. The former CEO of Netflix, Marc Randolph, was the keynote speaker. He offered tidbits learned from his experience to budding entrepreneurs in the audience.

"Constantly disrupt yourself, or someone will do it for you," Randolph offered as advice. He said great entrepreneurs were not always A students or B students. Rather, they have a great tolerance for risk. Randolph said a simple twist makes an idea genius and cited post-it notes. But you must be able to hear a certain number of detractors criticize the idea.

"The important part is to believe in your idea and persist in the odds against it. Because who could have seen something like "The Blair Witch Project" being big?" He later said he was investing in a cannabis company and called it "damn fun to watch."

The infamous boxer and "The Hangover" star Mike Tyson has launched a company called the Tyson Ranch and promoted a rolling paper brand called Futurola at MJ Biz Con. His team gave out samples of cones that can be filled with cannabis for smoking. Futurola's booth was wide with a white platform and a massive TV screen that displayed an ad with Tyson and Futurola cones. A large crowd gathered when they heard he was going to be there. Staffers tried to keep the floor aisles clear when he arrived with his entourage.

With a white beard, he seemed a bit older and wiser than you might expect. He certainly did not seem like the boxer who is known for biting an ear. There was such hype and crowd around him that it was overwhelming. As the industry becomes more mainstream, one can expect to see more celebrity endorsements.

Tyson's company was just one of many that were exhibiting their wares in a wide range of booths on the floor. One company demonstrated the ability of cannabis to keep things cold by distributing free beer and hard cider. They were especially interested in the B2B market. Many machines were being displayed that cut flowers and would thus get rid of the "trimmigrants," people who go to Northern California to find work cutting up harvested flowers in the fall. They still need engineers and laborers, the vendor said, adding that trimming is a tedious job to do.

As the industry grows, so do the ancillary supporting institutions. For example, Oaksterdam University in Oakland, California, offers vocational training for those interested in careers in the cannabis industry.[117] Founded in 2007, it is becoming increasingly well-respected. Accredited colleges across the country have started offering proper courses on the nuances of cannabis.

An online cannabis class was offered by Raritan Valley Community College (RVCC) in New Jersey in June 2020 to prepare students for jobs in cannabis dispensaries and elsewhere in the industry.[118] The March 2020 class, which was the first time the cannabis class was offered, was completed in May 2020. It featured New Jersey cannabis leaders teaching students about the nuances of the industry. The effort to offer a cannabis class was spearheaded by Sarah Trent, CEO of Valley Wellness.

"I saw a need for individuals interested in working in a dispensary ...to have a way to learn more about the laws and science of medical cannabis and to understand the skills and knowledge that one would need to successfully seek employment," Trent said.

Besides those looking for jobs, the cannabis class is relevant for individuals that want to know more about the industry, science, products, and regulations. The June 2020 class was designed to be comparable to the class taught in March 2020. The March class did not count towards college credits.

It normally costs $500. However, the program is offering tuition waivers for veterans. It is offered through the RVCC Workforce Training Center. In general, the center instructs students for jobs in specific trades.

The cannabis class is unique, with multiple individuals teaching full sessions for the duration of the class. It is exceptional because there are only five classes within the course, each lasting about three hours. Thus, the course is not spread over the length of the traditional college semester. One did not have to be an enrolled student at RVCC to take the cannabis class. Thus, it is not in the traditional model of academia in contrast to the program at Stockton University, which teaches several cannabis classes that amount to a minor in Cannabis Studies offered to enrolled students.[119]

Day one of the class addresses clinical cannabis laws, rules, and regulations of the New Jersey Medical Marijuana Program (NJMMP) taught by Trent and Seth Tipton, co-chair of the Cannabis Law Special Committee of the NJ State Bar Association.

"Teaching and curating the class has been very rewarding," said Trent regarding the cannabis class thus far.

The curriculum includes the history of the plant, plant physiology, the basics of commercial growth, and the nature of manufactured cannabis products. The class then showcases the Endocannabinoid System (ECS). The nature of the dispensary system is fully explored. The final session is a review of the prior classes, how to find a job in the industry, and resume building tips.

CHAPTER 11
OPPORTUNITIES

Multiple entrances are open to those who want to work in the cannabis industry. Many people have remarked that due to the rapid pace of change in a short period, working in cannabis is like dog years. Because Canada has already legalized adult-use cannabis, many of the largest cannabis companies are Canadian or have strong Canadian ties. Many cannabis entrepreneurs spent time there learning the nuances of the industry and then came home. Some of the cannabis businesses across the country have ties to the more established markets of Colorado or California's medical market or the far older underground market. As time goes on, there will be more opportunities for cannabis businesses, especially in the fields of:

- Cultivation
- Manufacturing
- Retail Dispensary Services
- Delivery

A growing number of jobs are those working at the dispensaries themselves. Starting as a budtender makes sense in many ways. A budtender interacts with the customers and recommends strains for them to address their needs. Ideally, budtenders are knowledgeable about the different strains being sold in terms of how they were grown, their specific effects, and methods of ingestion. It involves far more than the average retail clerk, and it pays a bit more.

Being a grower involves a great deal of knowledge regarding the nuances of the plant, along with horticulture and botany in general. Master Growers in the industry are experienced, having grown cannabis for many years. They have spent hours cultivating their plants.[120] A position formerly outside the law, the best Master Growers are now awarded Cannabis Cups at public competitions for the best-grown strains or cultivars in the legalized states.

Master Growers are experts on the cultivation of cannabis. They usually have at least five years of experience growing different strains. Someone aspiring to be one should have a background in horticulture, botany, and agriculture, which likely includes some formal study. They must also understand the laws surrounding growing in the state in which they operate.

For those who are entrepreneurial, one of the issues is that to get a dispensary up and running, you usually need to raise a significant amount of capital, up to a few million dollars, if not more. Winning a license, in general, is exceedingly difficult. Building a closely-knit team to get to that point is not easy. Moreover, it is competitive because of the finite number of licenses. Many towns are reluctant to have a dispensary within their limits in general. Thus, having an experienced lawyer, lobbyist, and political connections can be valuable. As winning a license becomes more widespread, there will be more experts at winning them.

Many compare the current cannabis industry to the Gold Rush. In the Gold Rush, many people went west to California, where gold was discovered, thinking they would find gold. Few became truly wealthy. Many of those who did sold goods to the gold miners. Hence, in the Green Rush, the best way to build wealth is to sell the equivalent of "shovels and pickaxes." An often-cited example of the ancillary model in the original Gold Rush is Levi Strauss's blue jeans, which were designed to be sufficiently durable for miners working under harsh conditions.

Ancillaries are lucrative. They are less susceptible to the legal and financial issues that come with being a plant-touching business. Most cannabis industry experts say the best way to get into the industry is to leverage your existing experience and assets into an ancillary business. For example, a lawyer becomes a lawyer focused on cannabis. An accountant focuses on cannabis clients etc.

Some profitable ancillary businesses include:

- Lawyers
- Accountants
- Software
- Security
- Logistics

One of the qualities an entrepreneur needs is to be passionate about their endeavor. It is especially important because a nascent business will inevitably face difficulties, and passion is what gets an individual through difficult periods.

Harry Carpenter is one of the premier accountants in New Jersey's cannabis industry and a partner at the firm Citrin Cooperman. Before getting into cannabis, Carpenter followed the issue as it progressed. But the need for it hit home once.

"My friend's mother had MS, while we lived together, she passed away," Carpenter explained. "I found out that her husband was scoring cannabis on the black market, and that was the only thing that made her feel better with her MS. That really hit me."

He entered the cannabis industry when he came across an interesting business lead.

"Someone came to me with an opportunity. A person was looking to start a medical marijuana (or clinical cannabis) farm in Jamaica," Carpenter explained. He said he asked his boss if he could pursue the business, and he approved. The deal fell through, though, after the prospect couldn't figure out how to get the money back to the United States. Thus, many people are not fully prepared to get into the industry.

When another prospect approached Carpenter seeking advice, he received approval to seek other cannabis businesses. Soon afterward, Carpenter learned others at Citrin Cooperman were forming a cannabis advisory division. They were looking for leaders to launch it and thought of him.

"Everyone needs an accountant and an attorney. Certainly, when structuring it and setting it up," Carpenter said regarding a business' needs. He has a variety of clients, including digital marketing firms, hemp farms, CBD processors, retailers, investors, and entrepreneurs, among others.

"Now I get to work in an industry where I really like the people. I feel the appreciation," Carpenter said.

He said the best way to get into the industry is to attend events. He said at his first cannabis event he didn't know anyone.

"And now I'm happy to see friends and clients," Carpenter said.

The best route into the industry, Carpenter said, is to shift your assets and experience into cannabis. Firms that take on clients can easily pivot to cannabis. For example, a graphic designer can make a logo for a dispensary. Others have left corporate careers to start businesses, which can be tough. Starting a business is indeed risky.

"Some business owners do it on the side. But you often need a big bank account to fall back on," Carpenter noted. It is popular to run a business on the side. Many entrepreneurs who run small businesses seek to bootstrap, which means using mostly their own money and credit cards for start-up capital. People will also seek loans or offer equity for cash from friends and family because you usually need to spend money to make money. As the business grows, they can bring on assistants or otherwise seek to scale or grow the business.

"It's like any industry that needs proper internal control, managing cash, bookkeeping, budgeting, security, and even a warehouse manager," Carpenter said regarding the opportunities.

Another way into cannabis is to get involved in a license application. For example, some license participants offer equity for services instead of payment. Those who help design retail spaces and security systems are highly valued. One could just invest in a business for a few years and earn a return on the investment or sell the shares after a few years and even potentially earn a higher return on the investment.

Carpenter explained the most lucrative opportunities are the riskiest. For example, in New Jersey, where getting a license is exceedingly difficult, you can make great profits if you get one. A business might not pay off in the first year due to start-up costs, especially for a dispensary, Carpenter noted. There is also a lot of uncertainty because the industry is new. Also, cannabis businesses have a higher risk of being audited than those in other industries. Plan Bs are good to have in multiple situations that could occur.

"Avoid putting all your eggs in one basket. Then you have flexibility and options," Carpenter said. "People should take their time and think major issues over," he added. An individual initially might want to be involved one way and then seek a different avenue. Educating yourself on the industry's nuances is also important.

Carpenter noted that the Multi-State Operator (MSO) Harborside was audited and had to pay $11 million to the IRS because they kept inaccurate records. Carpenter referred to as the "legacy mentality" of businesses not taking steps to comply with the law. Harborside considered that a win since they almost had to pay $90 million.

Section 280E of the tax code, which does not allow plant-touching businesses to deduct their expenses from their taxable income, is especially impactful on cannabis businesses. It adversely impacts their cash flow, partners, and tax liability. A lot of businesses in the industry pay an extremely high tax rate because they cannot write off expenses.

Section 280E was instituted because a drug dealer named Jeffery Edmondson initially won a court case in 1981, where he argued it was legal for him to deduct the expenses from running his illegal drug business and thus lessen his tax burden.[121] The following year in 1982, Congress passed "tax code 280E, banning businesses that trafficked Schedule I or Schedule II substances from taking business expenses besides the cost of goods sold."

Carpenter said misinformation is also a major challenge for businesses. It can be confusing what is legal, what is allowed in which state, and what the federal government allows. For example, a few professionals advised their clients that the 280-E issue did not apply to sales of CBD in 2018, before the implementation of the Farm Bill, which legalized hemp and CBD when it did indeed apply.

CHAPTER 12
GREEN ENTREPRENEURS

The entrepreneurs pioneering the cannabis industry are part of what makes it great. Dahlia Mertens has been building her cannabis topicals business, Mary Jane Medicinals, since 2009, and has seen a lot of change in the industry. Mertens was initially involved in the theater until she moved to the small town of Telluride, Colorado, in the southwest part of the state and became a massage therapist. A few years later, she visited her friend's cannabis farm in California to help trim. While there, she was offered a neck rub with infused oil. Mertens noted it felt great since cannabis oil is effective in relaxing muscles.

So, when she returned to Colorado, she started producing infused massage oil, making her business one of the first to sell cannabis topicals. When she started using the oil on her massage clients, they came back raving about how much better they felt afterward.

Mertens built her cannabis topicals business from the ground up with a mere $1,500 investment. She said $500 went to a friend for branding, and the rest was spent on ingredients and containers. She initially traveled door to door around the state, seeking to sell her product to medical dispensaries and giving out samples before she was able to sell products. At first, people were skeptical. But the product's effectiveness led many to call her back interested in retailing her product.

Mary Jane's Medicinals cannabis topicals are now being distributed in medical and adult-use dispensaries in Colorado, Oklahoma, and

New Mexico, among other places. Her best customers are baby boomers and seniors since they have the most aches and pains. They are not interested in smoking or edibles, but this is especially effective for them. It is especially interesting since a great deal of opposition to cannabis comes from older individuals. Athletes also like its healing power after working out.

Mertens said her cannabis topicals effectively relieve symptoms from arthritis, chronic pain, injuries, and skin conditions such as eczema and psoriasis. Mary Jane Medicinals offers a range of topical cannabis products to address pain, including salves, aloes, lotion, soap, topical tinctures, and massage oil. Her cannabis topicals contain both THC and CBD together, which makes her products more effective. While it does have THC, it is important to note that you cannot get high off a topical. She believes topicals are wonderful ambassadors to those skeptical of cannabis.

"Old folks love it," she noted, adding that her hometown mayor used the cream to heal a large scar from surgery to the point where it was barely visible after he used her oil for a month.

Conservatives who were wary of selling cannabis have begun to appreciate that it helps those seeking to cope with opioid addiction, along with its healing powers. Opioid addiction makes an individual mentally confused, nauseous, tired, and constipated. Those addicted to opioids find that cannabis lessens the harsh side effects of withdrawal, controls their cravings, and better manages existing pain.[122]

"The environment is changing. When I started back in 2009, it was just small business owners that were courageous enough to dive into the industry or had a good idea," Mertens said.

"None of us knew what we were doing," Mertens added, regarding the industry and regulators. "Sometimes, I thought I knew more than they did."

Since it is her first enterprise, Mertens said she has grown along with her business. She added that big money (banks and large businesses) changed the culture in Colorado. "It's good that small businesses are able to access funding easier," she said. Mertens said that the highly regulated nature of some of the new state markets would have made it difficult for an entrepreneur such as herself, to compete. She espoused a belief that free a market dominated by small businesses leads to a range of products.

Mary & Main is a medical marijuana dispensary founded by Hope Wiseman. Wiseman became the youngest black woman to win a dispensary license in 2016. She founded the dispensary with her mother, Dr. Octavia Wiseman, along with Dr. Larry Bryant, both dentists. Their dispensary is in Capitol Heights, MD. They first applied for a license in November 2015, won in 2016, and opened in 2018.

Wiseman is very active in the cannabis industry. Since winning the dispensary license, she has spoken on many panels at prominent cannabis conferences. On 4/20/2020, Wiseman hosted a virtual 4/20 conference that featured leaders discussing their expertise in the industry along with practical skills like how to roll a joint. She is also the Director of the Maryland Chapter of Minorities for Medical Marijuana (M4MM), which advocates for equitable legalization and educates people of color seeking to enter the industry.

Mary and Main provides premium quality products to patients at their dispensary with exemplary customer service. They pride themselves on their background in medicine, which gives them the ability to service those suffering from severe diseases. The company also holds educational events for patients about the nuances of the plant. Mary and Main has also held mindful meditation sessions in the dispensary. While many dispensaries are unable to find a bank to work with, Mary and Main found one, albeit with some difficulty. The dispensary vends many different cannabis brands and is listed as one of the top 10 dispensaries in Maryland.

"It's been really exciting," Wiseman said.

The company literally has social justice in its mission statement, saying, "We also strive to be active agents within our community through social action, cannabis education, and philanthropy to further educate others on the benefits of this alternative medicinal approach to health."[123]

Last year Wiseman and the dispensary held an almost five-month apprenticeship program for 20 individuals interested in getting into the cannabis industry. She wants to turn it into a statewide program and have direct access to jobs.

Wiseman's journey started in 2014 when she wanted to get into the industry. At the time, the mainstream media began discussing medical marijuana more, including Dr. Sanjay Gupta, who made a documentary that aired on CNN about cannabis.[124]

"I really fell in love with the science behind the plant and how it gives people medical relief," Wiseman said. Plus, she realized it would be one of the fastest-growing opportunities of her generation, an opportunity to get in on the ground floor. However, getting a license was an intense struggle. There were long delays in the application process. In their quest to build a great application, her team faced many hold-ups due to real estate and zoning issues.

Regarding those seeking dispensary licenses, Wiseman said, "It's nothing you can do overnight. You have to be in it for the long haul and have to have capital to be able to withstand the wait." Like many who have gotten a license, she advises Green Rushers to seek opportunities in the industries that are ancillary to cannabis, believing them to be easier to excel in.

Evan Nison is a New Jersey-based cannabis industry leader and advocate known within the industry and legalization movement nationwide. He is the youngest board member of NORML and sits on the NJ CAN 2020 steering committee, which seeks to legalize cannabis via the ballot referendum on November 3, 2020. His interest in cannabis reform was sparked in high school when he was subjected to a mandatory drug test, before being examined, when he went to the nurse due to stomach pain.

"It pissed me off. They prioritized a drug test over trying to make me feel better," Nison said. The equation of cannabis to heroin by authority figures and DARE also outraged him. While studying at Ithaca, he learned more about the nature of the War on Drugs and its negative impact.

He decided to run a ballot initiative in his hometown of East Brunswick, NJ, and neighboring New Brunswick in 2008. So Nison called NORML headquarters in Washington. Founder and current Legal Counsel Keith Stroup answered. Stroup walked Nison through the process, and from there, he became involved with NORML. His efforts were unsuccessful in both towns. Nonetheless, he remained committed to legalization.

In 2010 while still in college, he moved to California to organize in favor of the Prop 19 ballot referendum that almost legalized adult-use cannabis. Nison explained it was initially thought of as a joke.

"We took the conversation from "if" to "when and how," he said. Nison explained that they built support by highlighting that those in favor of cannabis reform were women and authority figures such as police and judges instead of young guys who just wanted to get high.

Nison said that those opposed to Prop 19 realized that they could not win claiming that legalization was bad and should not take place. Instead, the opposition found fault with specifics in the bill, which they used to campaign against legalization. Many of the issues they brought up were overblown or addressed in the bill. Even if advocates create the perfect bill, the opposition will find some fault with it, which will open it up to attack, Nison added. Prop 19 ended up receiving only 46.5 percent of the vote. Nison is worried that prohibitionists will do something similar in New Jersey in the November 2020 referendum.

Nison noted that the effects of the pandemic might change how the referendum campaign unfolds. Voter turnout may be affected, especially if life is not back to normal. The mainstream media probably will not allocate as much front-page news as it would have otherwise. However, there a couple of ways to campaign virtually Nison noted, such as a Reddit AMA and telephone town halls. The fact that cannabis is considered essential could have an impact on society's view of the issue.[125]

After Prop. 19, Nison lobbied for cannabis reform in New York and New Jersey. From these efforts, he found his first client and built the PR firm Nison Co. which works with cannabis-related businesses across the country. The firm and Nison himself are consistently ranked at the top of the cannabis industry.

Along with Nison Co., he started a business called Emerald Farm Tours, which runs outings of growing operations within the renowned growing region of the Emerald Triangle in Northern California. He also owns smoke shops with a friend who spent time in prison for cannabis. At times, he is amazed at how much has happened in the last ten years of cannabis.

"I never thought there would be an industry," Nison admitted. He said he has always been primarily concerned with legalization from a social justice point of view. Nison noted that few straddle both the cannabis industry and advocacy.

"The movement is skeptical of the industry, and the industry is not that interested in the movement. I try to do both the best as I can," Nison said. He argued that socially conscious entrepreneurs such as himself could change the nature of the industry by engaging with it.

"I'd rather have an industry of advocates instead of *vice versa*," Nison said. "This is the first industry I can think of literally born of a social movement. Industry was a minor thought of the advocates. I really hope that it does not lose that. I'm hoping as we build it, it keeps the social justice within it."

"To get the access to sit at the tables, I've sat at it, and while it has gone taboo to mainstream, you can't describe it. It's like a movie," he said.

Tara "Misu" Sargente has seen the cannabis industry transform from being underground to nearly legal in New Jersey. While doing so, she has made herself known nationally with her company Blazin' Bakery. It began when she was dating someone who could not drink but still wanted to have fun. So, she made pot brownies. When they turned out well, she offered them to friends who shared them with their friends. Thus, there seemed to be a market. However, she was wary of selling drugs. But selling the mix was appealing. So Misu researched the market and spent time perfecting her recipe. When she felt it was ready, Misu made a YouTube video about it, which went viral.

"It just grew from there," Misu said. She earned the nickname "Tara Misu" when her then-boyfriend named her after the dessert.

"I'm an Italian girl in Jersey that was baking, and my lawyer advised me not to use my real name. I liked it, and it stuck," Misu explained. Because she got into the industry before Colorado became the first state to legalize, she is justified saying, "I come from old school cannabis." A sign of how things have changed in cannabis was that Misu used to have dreadlocks.

"It was a different time. It added legitimacy," she explained, acknowledging how different the industry is now. "I never shy away from it." To establish her name in the industry, Misu hit the road.

"Conferences back then were very different. Back then, if you walked into a conference in a suit, they would have thought you were a cop," she said. Misu ended up spending six months out of the year traveling and promoting her brand.

"I'm a Jersey girl at heart, but I was on the road quite a bit," Misu said. A sign of how the travel paid off was that someone who complimented her brand heard of it while in Vancouver.

"Spencer's helped with that a lot. I was uniquely positioned with that," she said regarding the popular mall chain. Through her diligence, she was able to get a contract to provide brownie mixes to Spencer's stores in malls across the United States.

But the journey has not been easy. Despite having her product sold in malls, Misu's bank account has been closed twice. A bank once said, "You have to leave. We don't deal with your type of business."

Misu had to end her contract with Spencer's in 2014 because she could not meet the demand. The only investor she found that would have allowed her to scale was based in Colorado and required her to leave New Jersey, which she was not prepared to do. Spencer's now sells a knock-off made in China. She bares them no ill will, though.

In terms of her own business' future, she said, "I'm thinking way past brownies. That was cutting edge then. I just have a million ideas," she said. However, getting money to implement ideas still is not easy.

"It's harder for a woman. Ninety-seven percent of venture funding goes to white males," she said. Nonetheless, Misu is dauntless.

"I'm excited to get to expand Blazin' Bakery. I want it in every state. I've been called Betty Chronic," she said, a play on the well-known baking goods brand Betty Crocker. Before getting into the cannabis industry, she worked in marketing in the fashion business. Misu believes her marketing experience gives her an edge in cannabis.

"A lot of the cannabis marketing is homogenous, the names sound the same, there's not much thought put it into it," she noted.

Warren Bobrow is one of the premier cannabis mixologists in the country. His eventful career in the cannabis industry has led him to travel across the United States. At one point, Bobrow moved to Portland, Maine, where he worked in restaurants and became a chef as well as an excellent bartender. While a bartender, he became a great mixologist, specializing in creating unique alcoholic drinks.

After becoming a well-known mixologist, he wrote a book called "Bitters and Shrub Syrup Cocktails." He went to the New Orleans Pharmacy Museum to promote the book and was amazed to learn about the early medical role of cannabis.

"I had a dream in New Orleans, and I saw it. It was so profound," Bobrow said about the power of cannabis to heal people. It prompted him to begin looking into creating cannabis cocktails and mocktails. He had already been a fan of it for some time.

"Weed is exceptional. It makes you feel better about grim circumstances surrounding you," Bobrow said. "The only thing that kept me sane when working for a private bank was smoking cannabis."

Cannabis has also helped him medically. Bobrow learned he had glaucoma when the pressure in his eyes dropped, causing severe pain. He believes that he almost lost his vision and driving privileges. Bobrow explained that glaucoma is asymptomatic, meaning you do not know you have the condition until you have almost lost your sight if you have not been tested. At one point, he was taking a bottle of Advil every month because of the pressure. Finally, a doctor prescribed cannabis. That preserved his sight when, in 2015, he helped Bobrow get into the medical marijuana (or clinical cannabis) program.

Bobrow now specializes in making infused cannabis mocktails. A mocktail by law cannot contain alcohol. Instead, it includes a cannabis resin, which has a three-minute onset. He noted it is extremely predictable in terms of how it acts in contrast to edibles. In mocktails, the THC does not pass through one's liver like an edible, which takes time. Rather you feel the effect fairly immediately. One of Bobrow's favorite mocktail creations is a Vietnamese ice coffee with THC-infused condensed milk.

"It is just delicious in hot weather," Bobrow said. "It's a great summer drink, rich, refreshing, creamy, a little bitterness, a little sweet, like life itself." He added that because condensed milk is rich and dense, it works well in the drink.

Another drink he is proud of is the Mezzrow, named after the previously noted jazz musician Milton Mezzrow, who sold cannabis to Louis Armstrong, among others. The Mezzrow cocktail is comparable to a Manhattan drink, though with THC-infused vermouth. It contains sweet vermouth, cherries, and bourbon in a libation that Bobrow calls "deeply healing." The Mezzrow has sweet and sour cherries that complement its oaky flavor. He suggested the Cherry pie cannabis strain specifically to infuse it. The recipe is detailed in his book, "Cannabis Cocktails, Mocktails and Tonics, the Art of Spirited Drinks and Buzz-Worthy Libations."

Since getting into cannabis professionally, Warren Bobrow has written, by his estimation, several thousand articles for magazines and encyclopedias. He helped contribute to a book called "Higher Etiquette" by Lizzy Post, the granddaughter of Emily Post, who founded a school on etiquette.

In 2019, he created an infused craft mocktail using nanotechnology called Klaus after a gnome he owns. Before COVID-19, he said it was scheduled to be available in California dispensaries by April 20, 2020. The ingredients are a trade secret.

Bobrow travels all around the country to promote his business, visiting the legalized states of California and Oregon frequently. He regularly attends events like the Emerald Cup in California. Bobrow spoke at the Benzinga conference in Miami in February 2020. Also, he travels internationally.

"I smoked a J in Red Square," Bobrow said. "And not many people can say that."

Bobrow said he is well-known for his role in the cannabis industry in the western legalized states. He said individuals periodically stop him in the streets of San Francisco, Portland, Los Angeles, and Denver.

"I've done everything," he said regarding his career in the industry. "They say I have a great face for radio."

Regarding what he would like cannabis to be like, he said, "In the future, I would like to see cannabis de-stigmatized with more social acceptance, so I could walk outside and smoke a joint, and not get nasty looks," Bobrow said. "You don't get a nasty look for having a beer."

Gaetano Lardieri is leveraging his background in the pharmaceutical industry to change cannabis science through his company THCBD. While well-versed in the nuances of science after working in the field for years with professionals, he does not claim to be a scientist and does not hold a Ph.D. nor MD himself.

"I'm a project manager," he said. "I had to herd them like cats at times," he said regarding highly intelligent medical professionals.

Over his career, he consulted for many of the large pharmaceutical corporations in New Jersey in cancer research, often by running clinical trials. However, after years of doing so, Lardieri wanted to take a break. At first, he wanted to take a step back from cancer research and see what cannabis had to offer. He had become interested in the idea of cannabis being used to treat pain effectively. So, he decided to take a year and immerse himself in the nascent field.

"One year turned into five!" said Lardieri. What made cannabis science stand out to him was despite its murky status, it was that he had heard stories of people using it effectively to cope with pain.

"That always sat in the back of my head," Lardieri said. So, he threw himself into learning about the nuances of cannabis science and the industry. He became interested in the work of Israeli scientist Dr. Raphael Mechoulam. Mechoulam discovered the key chemical compound Tetrahydrocannabinol (THC), the chemical in cannabis that gets users high.[126]

While researching Mechoulam, he became interested in another Israeli cannabis science study. In it, a clinical trial for medicine was performed. While it initially showed positive results, they could not be repeated. That puzzled Lardieri. So, he began to interview master growers, experts on growing cannabis, on the nuances of the study. Lardieri ultimately concluded that, unfortunately, because cannabis is a plant, it cannot be perfectly replicated every time the way medicine is with every tablet being the same.

"You need to synthesize, to make sure these compounds are safe and efficacious for everyone," Lardieri explained. He believes a lot of cures can be derived from cannabis molecules once it is synthesized. So, he decided to launch his company, THCBD, to create synthetic cannabis that could be used to produce more effective medicine and products.

"It reminds me of oncology research 40 years ago," Lardieri said. "There's big things to be done with cannabis once it's descheduled, and we can study it properly," Lardieri added he has been in contact with prominent scientists. They would like to study cannabis but cannot due to issues stemming from its legal status.

Currently, only a limited amount of exceedingly poor-quality cannabis is available for scientists to study legally. Last October, a company called EPM, together with Dr. Mechoulam, synthesized synthetic cannabis acids. Lardieri said many companies are using a natural compound such as yeast, bacteria, or algae to replicate cannabis. However, this is difficult to do.

In stark contrast, THCBD is developing a process by which they can create the precursor compounds to produce cannabinoids using nanoparticles, which are inert material/carriers/vehicles. Lardieri believes their process will be more cost-effective and efficient to make cannabis medicine and products. He is currently preparing a pitch to investors. If interested, they would be required to sign a Non-Disclosure Agreement (NDA) before hearing the pitch. Hopefully, one of those hearing the pitch will want to invest in THCBD.

Lardieri is also involved in a firm with two scientists, which is experimenting with CBD, among other materials, to see if it can protect people from radiation, especially astronauts and others exposed to radiation due to their profession. They presented their proposal before a panel of NASA scientists in hopes of securing a grant. Lardieri explained that if a company is funded, NASA gives them technology and expertise to assist in experiments as well. The company keeps the Intellectual Property (IP) as they develop the product, and then an agreement is signed by which NASA can use it for the space program.

Since thousands are cut before that stage, Lardieri said he

considered it an honor simply to present. He added that it was quite an experience to be in a room full of literal rocket scientists presenting calculus formulations as if it were basic math. They also gave a similar presentation before an Assembly of the Committee on Space Research (COSPAR) in Australia. While cannabis science is his passion, Lardieri is no less devoted to full cannabis legalization.

"Keeping it in Schedule I is a prohibition against science, from studying it the right way," he said.

Lardieri said that he actually started advocating on cannabis reform and then figured how to turn it into a business.

"I'm all for erasing all the War on Drugs bullshit," Lardieri said, regarding the need to grant justice to those harmed.

In addition to his time developing THCBD, he has been a great advocate for cannabis reform. Lardieri joined the advisory board of the Coalition for Medical Marijuana of New Jersey (CMMNJ) in 2018. He has been working with others previously mentioned, including Ken Wolski, Jim Miller, and others for reform, including home cultivation of cannabis, better known as homegrow. He has personally spoken at events to State Senators to advocate for social justice and cannabis research.

While some are worried about the influence of Big Pharma on cannabis, Lardieri believes Pharma is not interested in growing cannabis, but rather wants to synthesize it to make the medication. His understanding of the best way to get health insurance companies to pay for cannabis drugs is through positive cannabis clinical trials.

Stu Zakim is a long-time aficionado of cannabis. Throughout his career, he has been in Public Relations for Universal Pictures, Rolling Stone, and Playboy.

"I've been very lucky that every job I've had was in a place... with a culture that doesn't inhibit me in my behaviors," Zakim said, regarding his consumption of cannabis.

He believed in the benefits and used cannabis for many, many years. Zakim does not believe cannabis to be a drug, but rather a plant. "Rolling Stone was my favorite job, rock, and roll, amazing," Zakim recalled. Through his work, he met a ton of people, including many of his idols. He was also able to smoke cannabis with a lot of interesting people in the late 80s. At the time, the atmosphere was like the freewheeling culture portrayed in the film *Almost Famous*. He also met some of their most famous writers, including Hunter S. Thompson and Kurt Loder, who became famous on MTV.

While working for Universal, Stu Zakim promoted the classic stoner film *Half Baked*. He was a great fan of the film from the start. He recounted riding NJ Transit and reading the script on the way home, laughing hysterically. *Half Baked* stars Dave Chapelle and Jim Brewer were in New York, where Zakim was based. They used to hang out in his office and get high in the bathroom. While the film did not initially make much money, it has become a cult classic. The coolest people Zakim said he ever smoked with were Cheech and Chong themselves.

Given his time in the film industry, Stu Zakim has been a member of the Academy of Motion Picture Arts and Sciences, which awards the Oscars, since 1995. Zakim worked in publicity at Showtime when the hit show *Weeds* debuted. Starring Mary-Louise Parker as Nancy Botwin, the show was about a single mother who sold cannabis to support her family after the death of her husband. Stu Zakim said it was ahead of its time. It was the first TV show to celebrate cannabis and illustrate how a single mom could make money.

Zakim's formal entry into the cannabis industry more directly came when, six years ago, a friend launched the Seattle-based Marijuana Business Association (MJBA), as the Washington State legal market was about to open. Many people wanted to get into the industry but didn't know what to do, so Zakim helped develop and promote educational panels on the nuances of the industry.

Zakim sought to bring MJBA to the New York market, which was difficult because the medical marijuana market was not very large, which meant that there was insufficient demand to keep it afloat in New York. However, Zakim met many people through the MJBA and through advocacy. With his connections, he launched his public relations firm, Bridge Strategic Communications.

Zakim is especially adamant about erasing the old stigma associated with consuming cannabis. Thus, he thinks it important to portray regular cannabis users as fully functional, not sitting around in a daze as media often does.

"You change perceptions if seemingly normal people admitted they smoke," Zakim said.

Jesse Villars is a testament to the healing power of cannabis and the industry's ability to pay it forward to those suffering.

"I started as a patient in Medical Marijuana for five years; there have been many benefits. I started making my own edibles, and people liked it. And then I got involved in a store," Villars said regarding her own experience.

She now manages a CBD catering business called Baked by the River with her boyfriend, Cord Schlovohm, which specializes in infused desserts. Branded as "CBD Bakers," her products include a wide variety of cakes, cookies, pies, pastries, and muffins. Villars is planning to get into adult-use cannabis infusion when that becomes legal. When baking, Villars often uses coconut oil, olive oil, and butter to make meals for patients, like a CBD dinner or dessert, which is her specialty. She said she likes three-tier lemon coconut cake the best, along with devil's food chocolate cake with peanut butter mousse filling and chocolate ganache.

"I've always loved baking as a coping mechanism. It's been incredibly beneficial," Villars said. She noted that under the law, she cannot make adult-use edibles. Villars does, however, make medical marijuana infusion tutorials and baked edibles for patients using their prescription mixed into coconut, butter, or olive oil. Coconut is best when baking strong THC edibles because it has a high saturated fat content and absorbs more than butter.

Villars is sensitive to those with dietary restrictions, saying, "we work with gluten-free, sugar-free, pescatarian, vegetarian and vegan diets." She added that she uses rice flour and almond flour gluten-free alternatives.

Villars and her boyfriend have been together four years and work together at Baked by the River. She said they work well together because she has a mild disability, so heavy lifting and chopping are more difficult for her.

"We love it. Unless I leave dirty dishes in the sink but there's edibles, so it's all good in the end," she joked.

When they met, "We were both opioid addicts and getting sober at the same time... so we were the only two trying to stay away, clean on our own terms, and we helped each other in that first year. It was a perfect time to find each other because we needed to lean on each other and a medical marijuana prescription to stay clean," she noted.

Villars believes that edibles are the healthiest method of consumption, especially for those seeking to avoid inhaling smoke.

"I'd like to work with medicine dispensaries to get referrals for alternative options for medicine," she said.

She is planning to do more on CBD education courses since the demand is so high. Villars is especially interested in treating specific ailments such as cancer with cannabis and making topical creams.

CHAPTER 13
LEGAL STATUS

D espite the industry's exponential growth, the legal status of cannabis markets is precarious. While legal on the state level in certain states, cannabis is still illegal on the federal level. It has led to many raids by the Drug Enforcement Agency (DEA) and federal crackdowns, even in legalized states. Cannabis' federally illegal status was especially problematic in the early days of the medical marijuana programs, where the DEA did not recognize the validity of the states' laws. It made operating in the medical cannabis industry especially difficult.

During the Obama Administration, the Ogden memo issued by the Justice Department told U.S. Attorneys not to prioritize fighting medical marijuana programs.[127] The implementation of the Ogden memo allowed the Colorado medical marijuana program to grow to five times its initial size, from less than 20,000 patients to 100,000 patients in a year. In 2013 the Cole Memo prevented the Justice Department from interfering in states where adult-use cannabis had been legalized.[128] The Cole Memo has allowed adult-use cannabis markets to flourish.

However, when Donald Trump appointed Jefferson Beauregard "Jeff" Sessions as Attorney General, the regulatory environment became less friendly when he rescinded the Cole Memo.[129] As a Republican Senator from Alabama, Sessions was a leading prohibitionist. However, he was not Attorney General long enough to inflict, as he had hoped to do, lasting damage to the cannabis industry. His successor, Bill Barr, thus far has been more favorable to its existence. Barr testified before Congress that he would not interfere with businesses in compliance with state cannabis laws.[130]

However, he has been problematic, as well. In June 2020, a Department of Justice (DOJ) official testified before Congress that Barr wasted department resources targeting cannabis companies for anti-trust infringement because he did not like them.[131] Barr had been pursuing furthering the Trump administration's political goals using the DOJ and fighting cannabis reform. The House Judiciary Committee held a very contentious hearing on the issue of Barr using the DOJ for political ends and his interference in cannabis company mergers.

John W. Elias, a DOJ official in the anti-trust division, testified on the issue of Barr using the DOJ to target cannabis companies. Elias said the Justice Department reviews a small amount of anti-trust cases. Of the cases that are reviewed, cannabis companies take up almost a third. Elias cited the MedMen and PharmaCann merger, which was the first deal they specifically examined. The deal was ultimately so delayed it was called off. Nine other mergers were investigated. No real issues were found since these companies did not compete against each other. At one point, an office handling the specifics of the investigation was so inundated due to orders from Barr they had to get staff from another part of the DOJ to handle the requests.

"Cannabis is unpopular on the fifth floor," Elias said, referring to Barr's office.

Elias argued there was never ground to base anti-trust investigations.

For all the problems with the Multi-State Operators (MSOs), there certainly are no monopolies. None of them could claim to be as ubiquitous as Walmart, Amazon, or Facebook.

Elias said he reported these issues to the Inspector General, who is empowered to deal with internal issues such as these.

"I have undertaken whistle blower...activity because there is evidence our nation's anti-trust laws are being abused," Elias said. This is not the first-time anti-trust laws have been abused. In the past, they were used against labor unions and similar organizations of workers banding together. The Justice Department has been used many times throughout its history to suppress radicals.

Every year since 2014, a rider called the Rohrabacher-Farr amendment, which prevents the Justice Department from interfering in the legal medical cannabis states, had been inserted into the federal budget.[132] A rider is a unique legislative provision that has worked to protect the markets so far. The Rohrabacher-Farr amendment has allowed medical marijuana programs and the dispensaries that serve patients across the United States to grow steadily without fear of being shut down by the DEA. But because such initiatives can easily be reversed, the regulatory framework establishing the market for the nascent industry is unstable at best.

Thankfully for cannabis advocates, Congress has become more friendly to cannabis, especially the Democratic-controlled House. In 2019, the United States House of Representatives approved an amendment to the federal budget that prohibits the DOJ from cracking down on state-legal recreational marijuana programs.

Congressman Earl Blumenauer (D-OR), a longtime supporter of cannabis legalization, spoke in favor of the bill during a House floor debate declaring, "This is what the American people have demanded, why it is now legal in 33 states. It is supported by two-thirds of the American public, and 90 percent for medical marijuana. It's time that we extend this protection to state-legal activities, so they can drive and move forward."[133]

The historic nature of the U.S. House vote on marijuana reform cannot be overemphasized.

"Today's action by Congress highlights the growing power of the marijuana law reform movement and the increasing awareness by political leaders that the policy of prohibition and criminalization has failed."

Because the amendment passed as part of a yearly spending bill, it would have had to be approved the following year again to remain in effect, a practice not uncommon in Congress. Unfortunately, it was not approved by the Republican-controlled Senate in the first place.

Leave it to the States

The continued growth of the U.S. cannabis market relies on the federal legalization of cannabis. One way to protect the current markets is for Congress to pass the Strengthen the Tenth Amendment Through Entrusting States (STATES) Act. The bipartisan bill would allow state-legal marijuana markets to function without federal interference. This bill states that, like in the 10th Amendment in the Bill of Rights, in the United States, powers not delegated to the federal government are given to state governments. Thus, states should be allowed to legalize and regulate cannabis without fear of federal interference.

The STATES Act was introduced into the House by Blumenauer and Congressman David Joyce (R-OH) and in the Senate by Elizabeth Warren (D-MA) and Cory Gardner (R-CO). Donald Trump indicated he would support the STATES Act if Congress passed it.[134] Trump has not expressed a strong opinion on cannabis while in office. He seems to content to let it play out for now, though his opinion on issues often changes quickly.

Governors from 12 states sent a letter to Congress, urging the federal lawmakers to pass legislation that would allow states to manage marijuana laws within their respective borders without interference from the federal government. The Governors' marijuana letter was signed by the governors of California, Colorado, Maryland, Massachusetts, Nevada, New York, North Dakota, Oregon, Pennsylvania, Utah, Washington State, and Vermont. The Governors calling for cannabis reform have a variety of backgrounds and include both progressive Democrats and conservative Republicans.

"The STATES Act is a logical step for Congress because it honors state action by codifying protection at the federal level for those businesses and consumers operating in accordance with state law," their letter said. "The STATES Act is not about whether marijuana should be legal or illegal; it is about respecting the authority of states to act, lead and respond to the evolving needs and attitudes of their citizens."

The number of Governors that support marijuana has grown in recent years, as the medical and financial benefits of legalization have become more widely known, and cannabis gains popular support.

Local Control

Another legal issue facing the cannabis industry is that even in states where cannabis has been legalized, towns were allowed to ban the establishment of a dispensary within city limits. It is even an issue in California, where the underground market has been popular for years, and the movement for clinical cannabis began. According to a poll conducted by the UC Berkeley Institute of Government Studies, 68 percent of Californians approve of the legalization of recreational cannabis. Sixty-three percent said they want marijuana stores to be in their communities. When broken down on the local level, cannabis reform is popular across California, even in the more conservative Riverside and San Bernardino counties.

Despite widespread support for legalization, 75 percent of the municipalities in California have banned retail cannabis stores. Moreover, 24 such municipalities have been seeking to ban home deliveries from businesses based elsewhere through a lawsuit. Some towns were eager to see how a legal marijuana market played out in San Francisco and Los Angeles first. A few Californian cities have put the question on a local ballot initiative. In more progressive places such as Malibu and Pasadena, residents have voted in favor of allowing a marijuana retail store within their limits.

The 601 retail cannabis stores operating in California in 2019 is a far smaller amount than the initially predicted 6,000 dispensaries. Sales were estimated to reach $3.1 billion in 2019, which was lower than what experts had initially expected.[135] It is noteworthy that the majority of California's population lives in the 25 percent of towns where it is legal to sell cannabis.

It is an issue not only in California but in most of the states where cannabis is legal. Most of the more conservative rural towns have banned cannabis stores, including Colorado, where the movement for legal adult-use markets began.

CHAPTER 14

TAX REVENUE

One of the main reasons many states passed legalized cannabis was the prospect of a new tax revenue stream. The money collected could be used to fund critical infrastructure projects. It subsequently saves politicians from having to decide to raise taxes or cut programs. For states with balanced budget requirements on the books, that revenue is especially attractive. However, many states have imposed exceedingly high sales tax rates on cannabis.

Many consumers in California consider the taxes on marijuana purchases, which adds at least 15 percent to the cost, excessive. The high cost of legal cannabis has given many an incentive to continue purchasing their products from the underground market. That contributed to the revenue from the California adult-use market falling short of the amount it was expected to generate.

A report from Pew Charitable Trusts in 2019 suggested that calculating revenue projections for legalized cannabis tax revenue are challenging.[136] Actual revenue often differs from initial expectations once adult, recreational cannabis use becomes law. In 2018, Nevada ended up collecting 40 percent more revenue than what was initially predicted. In comparison, California received 45 percent less than the amount analysts expected after their adult-use market opened. As the markets mature in Colorado and Washington, the first two states to legalize adult-use cannabis in 2012, cannabis tax revenue has been growing at a slower pace than in the markets' earlier years, which is logical. Because the nation's legal cannabis markets are so new, a lack of reliable data makes it challenging to predict revenue specifics.

"The difficulty in forecasting revenue is compounded by the fact that states have only recently begun to understand the adult-use cannabis market's nuances in terms of the level of consumer demand for recreational products, the types of users and how much they might pay, and competition with the black market," the report from Pew concluded. As the industry matures, more data will become available to study.

"The biggest hurdle for states is the lack of reliable data," explained Alexandria Zhang, one of the authors of the report.[137] Zhang added that part of the reason that California tax revenue fell so short of projections was that it had taken the state longer than expected for its legal market to begin operating. Also, the high fees companies must pay in California to comply with regulation have caused prices to be higher than expected. High prices are believed to be incentivizing consumers to purchase their cannabis products from the illegal market, reducing the amount of tax revenue the state derives from legal sales.

Alaska has allowed legal marijuana sales since October 2016. Ken Alper, former Director of Alaska's Department of Revenue, said the lingering stigma around cannabis use when it remains illegal contributes to the challenges of developing revenue estimates.[138] Potential consumers surveyed about prior cannabis use are more inclined to lie regarding their consumption habits.

The diversity of marijuana products that have sprung up in legalized markets also complicates the picture. Because these products are taxed at different rates for different products and in different states, it can be hard to estimate how much revenue will be earned. For example, in Colorado, edibles and cannabis concentrates have become popular, while in Washington, cannabis extracts are the top choices for consumers. These factors have made predicting a state's legal marijuana market difficult, often leading to unreliable calculations.

In Connecticut, where adult-use legalization was being debated in 2019 before COVID hit, budget analysts have predicted the state will receive $30.1 million in tax revenue from legal marijuana sales in the market's first year. Marijuana-legalization advocates, however, estimate that Connecticut could collect as much as $60 million in that first year.

While many consider the tax on cannabis in California to be high, state excise, and cultivation taxes increased in California at the beginning of 2020, a move some believed would be a blow to licensed businesses. The California Department of Tax and Fee Administration (CDTFA) announced it was raising taxes on wholesale cannabis products, including flowers and plants, to adjust for inflation.

The CDFTA is tasked with determining the average markup rate on cannabis taxes every six months to ensure that the tax paid is equal to 15 percent of the gross receipts, as required by California's adult-use marijuana law, Proposition 64.

According to the CDTFA's website, "an analysis of statewide market data was used to determine the average markup rate between the wholesale cost and the retail selling price of cannabis and cannabis products. Based on this analysis, effective January 1, 2020, the newest markup rate will be 80 percent."

California is home to the world's largest legal cannabis market, but the state's underground market is thriving. The latest tax increase will exacerbate price point discrepancies and potentially drive more consumers to the illegal market.

"Widening the price disparity gap between illicit and regulated products will further drive consumers to the illicit market at a time when illicit products are demonstrably putting people's lives at risk," the California Cannabis Industry Association (CCIA) wrote in response to the announcement.

"The reason the black market continues to exist is that taxes are too high," said Jay Handal, co-owner of Erba Markets, a Los Angeles-based dispensary. "People are looking for the best value, and the government, both state and city, are woefully poor at shutting down black market stores. Raising taxes will only exacerbate the situation by continuing to keep black market store prices markedly lower than legal dispensaries that carry tested products."

For consumers, "ultimately, they'll feel that at the register," Joshua Drayton of the United Cannabis Business Association said.

Californian legislators rejected a bill in spring 2019 that would have lowered the tax on cannabis. Under California's recreational use law, adults ages 21 years and older can possess up to 28.5 grams of marijuana and 8 grams of concentrated marijuana. Adults are also allowed to grow up to six plants.

CHAPTER 15

BANKING ISSUES

O ne of the most difficult issues for companies in the cannabis industry is how poorly most banks have reacted to legalization. Banks are wary of working with businesses in the industry because they could suffer heavy fines if found to be working with organized crime and laundering money.[139] Some cannabis companies can find a smaller bank or credit union to service them, but it is especially difficult if they have "cannabis" in their name, much less be a plant-touching business.

Thus, many dispensaries are forced to operate on a pure cash basis. Because they operate as cash businesses, processing payroll, and paying taxes along with other expenses are cumbersome and inefficient in the digital age. Keeping a lot of cash around also poses a great security risk. Thus, businesses must invest heavily in security cameras and guards.

Businesses in the industry also face challenges when seeking loans for expansion. Ancillary businesses providing services to plant-touching businesses are in danger of losing access to financial services since their banks are also susceptible to charges of money laundering. The inability to access formal banking services is impeding the industry's growth. While California is one of the oldest markets in the country, cannabis businesses face some of the strongest barriers to formal banking there. Meanwhile, banking has improved in New Jersey, where two community banks accept cannabis-related accounts. However, credit card processing is still a difficult issue for many, including CBD businesses.

"Unless you have deep pockets, money is an issue," said Harry Carpenter, a partner at the accounting firm Citrin Cooperman.

To address the issue, Congressman Ed Perlmutter (D-CO) introduced the Secure and Fair Enforcement (SAFE) Banking Act, which would enable access to banking in states where marijuana is legal. Legal marijuana banking would save the federal government $4 million over ten years. The bill passed the House Financial Services Committee in May 2019. The SAFE Banking Act passed the House of Representatives by a comfortable margin of 321-103 in October 2019.

"I want to thank all my colleagues who have listened to me talk about the need to address this problem for six-plus years as well as the staff and the coalition that came together to get this bill over the finish line in the House," Perlmutter tweeted.

The bill had a remarkable number of 206 bipartisan co-sponsors.[140] For reference, a majority in the House is obtained with 218 votes of the 435 Members. While most sponsors were Democrats, 16 were Republicans known for more moderate views or represent states where it is legal.

"The SAFE Act bill will [...] provide banking to the industry the way banking is done with other businesses," said Matthew Schweich, Deputy Director of the Marijuana Policy Project (MPP). Schweich added that the bill contained a provision that would assist people of color who have less access to private wealth.

He explained that on the state level, lawmakers are seeking to include such provisions in legalization bills.

"We at MPP will push for further reform," Schweich said, reasoning that momentum from the SAFE Act will help further bills and certainly not hurt their chances of passage.

The Republican-controlled Senate poses a challenge for reform because one senator can block the measure nearly indefinitely unless persuaded otherwise. While Republicans have warmed to cannabis reform due to its public support and the potential financial boom the industry can bring, Republican Senate leaders have not indicated they will offer legitimate support. It seems the opposite is true.

A coalition of many interest groups was formed to support the passage of the SAFE ACT. State Banking Associations in all 50 states and Puerto Rico urged the Senate to allow cannabis businesses full access to banks without repercussions. The state associations wrote a letter in support of the legislation that would allow financial institutions to service marijuana businesses without fear of federal repercussions.[141] The letter was addressed to the Senate Banking Committee, which has jurisdiction over the issue and must pass the bill before the full Senate can vote on it.

The coalition urged Banking Committee members to take action, saying they "support a thorough examination of the issue and potential legislative solutions by the committee. We appreciate that there are broader public policy questions surrounding cannabis legalization that merit debate, but we ask that you focus narrowly on the urgent banking problem at hand, which is within your power to resolve."

Support for the SAFE Act has also come from the Independent Community Bank Association (ICBA), which represents smaller banks, the National Association of State Attorneys General, and the National Association of State Treasurers, among other organizations. Thirty-eight state and territorial attorneys general have called on Congress to pass federal legislation that would allow marijuana businesses to access the federal banking system.

Banking Committee Chairman Mike Crapo (R-ID) has impeded the progress of the bill by refusing to hold a hearing to discuss it. He has opposed all types of cannabis reform. Crapo claims that the bill cannot go through because cannabis is illegal and must be dealt with by the Department of Justice first. His home state of Idaho is one of the states most opposed to legalization.

Even though the SAFE Act has not passed the Senate, it was a victory when it passed the House of Representatives. Many landmark bills had to be introduced multiple times before they were finally signed into law.

"Ten years ago, we could not get a single bill introduced into Congress, much less a hearing," Erik Altieri of NORML said.

While the issue remains unresolved, the number of banks working with marijuana businesses has increased as new legal markets open. A financial report released in 2019 showed that more banks and credit unions are doing business with firms in the cannabis industry, albeit quietly.[142] According to data released by the U.S. Treasury Department's Financial Crimes Enforcement Network (FinCEN), 493 banks and 140 credit unions were providing financial services to businesses in the marijuana industry as of March 2019. It was a 54% increase from the previous year when only 411 such institutions were doing so.

The data on FinCEN's website indicated that the financial institutions serving cannabis industry clients are in the Pacific Northwest, with an increasing number appearing in California. Credit unions typically have accepted many more cannabis business customers despite banks outnumbering credit unions in the U.S. Earlier data published in 2018 by FinCEN also showed a boost in the number of banks serving the cannabis industry.

The banks' fear of federal repercussions seems overblown since no bank has been prosecuted for doing business with a cannabis-based business. Moreover, the four largest banks in the United States have been doing business with cannabis-related businesses already; these include Bank of America, Citigroup, JP Morgan, and Wells Fargo. They have done business with a select number of companies, though they did not widely publicize the fact.

Financial experts have questioned whether the number of cannabis-supporting financial institutions is as high as data from FinCEN suggests. Tyler Beuerlein, Vice President of the Banking

Committee of the National Cannabis Business Association, said that these numbers are not accurate because they are based on Suspicious Activity Report (SAR) filings. When there is an institution affiliated with a cannabis business, a SAR is filed. Individuals businesses might have more than one SAR. If applying stricter criteria by which banks must have multiple cannabis-related clients and have dedicated resources to cultivating such business, Beuerlein believes the number of banks doing business with cannabis-related businesses is closer to 40.

He argued that while the FinCEN data suggests that financial institutions are accepting significantly more marijuana businesses, banks and credit unions might only be doing business with a few cannabis clients and not actively seeking to increase that number.

Criminal justice advocates are exceedingly critical of banking reform since it contains no provisions to assist those charged with possession. They say marginalized communities that bore the brunt of the War on Drugs have yet to reap the benefits of legalization.

CHAPTER 16
COMPLICATIONS

As the industry has grown, so have the problems within. The United Food and Commercial Workers (UFCW) union has been instrumental in securing legitimacy for the industry. At the same time, they have fought the worst aspects of the industry to help cannabis workers.

The UCFW started to advocate with cannabis workers in California in the early 2000s during the market's medical days. It was more of a movement then with the industry consisting of many small businesspeople focused on caring for patients. One of their locals (chapters) in the Bay area first formed a partnership with the movement. They liked cannabis and understood it from a social justice perspective. Through working with the UFCW, cannabis activists were able to secure meetings with high-level politicians to lobby them effectively. The UFCW saw the potential of the industry to create good jobs and address social justice issues. Thus, around 2012, they began organizing cannabis workers in California. The UFCW now represents about 10,000 workers in 15 states.

The UFCW's relationship with the industry soured in Colorado after the Cole Memo was issued, even though businessmen leaned on the UFCW to pass legalization. Previously, the UFCW's partnership had been with West Coast hippie types and people from the legacy market. The industry's treatment toward the UFCW is especially egregious because it was through the connection of one of their top lobbyists that the Cole Memo was issued. Their lobbyist had a strong relationship with Barack Obama, dating to his early days in Chicago. Thus, the Cole Memo protecting the legal adult-use markets was issued by Deputy Attorney General James Cole of the Justice Department in August 2013.

Corporate cannabis executives then came into the industry with backgrounds in real estate, law, or finance. These businessmen (and they were largely men) were interested in profit more than anything else. The UFCW official noted most of them paid lip service to progressive values, the benefit of labor unions, and the virtues of the plant before the passage of legalization. However, there was a change in attitude from the Multi-State Operators (MSOs) Curaleaf, Acreage Holdings, iAnthus, and MedMen, especially once legalization passed. A lot of these companies seem like they were explicitly designed to maximize profit at the expense of workers and social justice. They were not interested in building a lasting company or brand. A UFCW official called them "paper tigers."

The initial pioneers of the cannabis industry are mostly gone, the UFCW official said. They were driven out of business, left disgusted in how the industry developed or sold out.

In the early days, the UFCW saw cannabis workers were not getting paid, paid in cash or cannabis itself, and sexual harassment was common. Many came from the legacy market and did not have experience in a legitimate workplace. They were at the mercy of employers who took advantage.

Cannabis workers face the same issue as workers in other industries, such as disrespect, bad pay, and no health insurance. They face the issues experienced by Walmart workers who are often dependent on state benefits such as Medicaid and food stamps to make ends meet. When companies say they are bringing in great tax revenue to a state, they do not mention their workers are a drain on tax revenue because they do not compensate them adequately.

Cannabis workers specializing in growing plants face health and safety issues that are unreported. They often do not receive protective equipment nor safety training. Workers are often in environments polluted by chemicals that lead to deadly lung diseases.

The UFCW partnered with the health and federal safety regulators to study conditions in the industry. One study revealed that extraction facilities in which workers developed deadly lung disease have the worst working conditions. There is also the issue of fire safety. Cannabis extraction using butane is dangerous. Workers in extraction are untrained and poorly compensated.

"There is potential for real disaster," said a UFCW official.

The application of harmful pesticides to cannabis affects patients and consumers too. Many off the pesticides are illegal. Nonetheless, companies ignore safety regulations, which is harmful to patients, and the long-term health of workers. In Colorado, most of the companies were using the chemical fertilizer Eagle 20, which is banned in the U.S. because it causes sterility in men. The gray zone in which cannabis operates is not conducive to improving conditions. For example, it is difficult for MSOs to find quality health insurance. The plans for cannabis workers often only cover emergencies rather than the checkups covered by a sound plan.

"No doubt this industry is not what it needs to be for women and people of color," the UFCW official said.

Despite facing great issues, the UFCW has won victories for cannabis workers. The UFCW official described a successful campaign at Garden State Dispensary in Woodbridge, NJ, that helped a couple that met there and married. In 2016, they were making $13 an hour and scraping by with public benefits. They earned around $20 an hour in July 2020, along with a retirement plan and health insurance. They bought a house because the UFCW fought to make their jobs sufficient to sustain a middle-class lifestyle.

In January 2020, the cannabis workers of Cresco Labs in Joliet,

IL, won the largest National Labor Relations Board (NLRB) election in the industry where they voted overwhelmingly for the union. The UFCW also won an election at the Sunnyside dispensary in Chicago. In Massachusetts, they won an election at a Curaleaf dispensary. In July 2020, they won an election at the Mayflower Medicinals dispensary, a subsidiary of iAnthus in Massachusetts. One of the UFCW's advantages in organizing cannabis workers is that the majority are politically progressive and receptive to the union's message. Many supported Bernie Sanders' progressive platform or fought for social justice themselves.

There have been, of course, defeats. Many companies engage in union-busting tactics. In a dispensary in Brookline, MA NETA fired 53 people for forming a union. Because the Trump administration is against unions, the UFCW was wary of going to the NLRB to fight them. In New Jersey, there are strong protections within state law to which cannabis workers can turn for protection. If NETA were to fire 53 workers for unionizing in New Jersey, the MSO would lose their license.

A cannabis worker is often enthusiastic at working in the industry and initially accepts poor conditions. But after several months, they may become disillusioned and leave for a job that pays more or are fired. Thus, there is a high turnover. Also, many cannabis workers are scared of retaliation from the bosses and do not understand they can form a union.

Unfortunately, cannabis stocks performed poorly in 2019. The market prices declined between 2 and 17 percent after third-quarter results were released.[143] Part of the reason was a bubble built over time, and bubbles inevitably burst. Some believe the reason stocks did so poorly was that the California market is overtaxed to the point where negligible profits were gained from companies operating there. Others blame the vaping crisis for a decline in sales. The banking issue previously described, along with other issues stemming from federal prohibition, likely contributed to the bubble bursting as well.

Many experts believe that the industry was inundated with bad actors who sought to make a quick buck in cannabis or CBD due to the Green Rush. Some rushed to get into CBD and did not sell quality products. Since its legalization via the 2018 Farm Bill, CBD has become a booming business and a craze. It is now being sold at stores throughout the country. However, the CBD market is not well regulated. Thus, many feel many CBD products are sub-par, including placebos that are comparable to snake oil.

To better regulate the industry, in July 2019, the FDA issued a directive ordering CBD companies to stop making health claims regarding their products. Several prominent companies were sent warning letters regarding the health claims they had been making. It was done to eliminate the snake oil reputation of CBD. There is a great deal of anecdotal evidence that it is effective in treating ailments. (Buyer beware when purchasing CBD). Moreover, there have not been many scientific studies regarding CBD because cannabis is a Schedule I narcotic, which makes it difficult to research legally. The FDA is in the process of studying CBD and its effects.

According to M.J. Business Daily President Chris Walsh, while the legal cannabis industry looks healthy in the long-term, the tumultuous nature of the industry has hurt many of the prominent companies. Canopy Growth Corporation stock (CGC) was valued near $40 per share at its height, for example, and had dropped to $18 in December 2019. They are facing the issues many corporations are also dealing with, like being unable to write off expenses or receive a loan from a bank. In a bubble of investment, some said investment expectations were too high.

While some think that cannabis has unlimited potential, other experts warn that if it just becomes another commodity like apples, then there will not be much profit in it at all in the end. But others say it is more like wine, and wine is no simple commodity.[144] Others point to cannabis being refined into beverages or other products where it can be sold as a commodity comparable to wine rather than a pack of cigarettes.

Many other corporations in the tobacco, alcohol, and pharmaceutical industries are interested in getting into cannabis, including Altria (formerly Phillip Morris) and CVS. The issue with this is best illustrated in the story of Canopy Growth Corporation (CGC). Bruce Linton built CGC into the largest publicly traded cannabis company in the world. In 2018 Constellation Brands, an international producer of alcohol and Fortune 500 company, invested $4 billion into the Canadian-based company and acquired a controlling interest at 38 percent.[145]

Constellation was subsequently dissatisfied with the financial growth of Canopy Growth, which created tension. Soon after, Linton was forced out of the company. Constellation Brands was not without their reasons for wanting Linton to leave in July 2019. In the months before Linton left, the company lost millions of dollars. Due to legal hurdles, interstate commerce is exceedingly difficult. Also, Canada's total population is only 38 million, so they had a limited domestic market.

Linton showed little bitterness over his departure. Instead, he was philosophical about it. Linton thought a lot about his six years with Canopy in terms of what he learned and what he could have done better. After waiting, he announced he was going to become Executive Chairman of Vireo Health Inc., a medical marijuana Multi-State Operator (MSO) active in 11 states with 400 employees based in Minneapolis.

"My non-compete applies to Canada only and cannabis in Canada only," Linton said. He noted this allowed him to explore businesses elsewhere across the globe.

Before getting involved in the cannabis industry, Linton worked in the telecom and tech industries and founded several companies.

A native of Ontario, he founded CGC with a few others in 2013 as Tweed Marijuana Inc. Linton attributes his success in cannabis to being able to sum up his message and taking the risk of being an industry leader when few companies were seeking such a position. Medical marijuana became legal in Canada in 2001, but the industry struggled to grow. Linton described how he persuaded many people who were in their 40's and 50's that supporting the prohibition of cannabis was to support the black market and crime. Only a criminal would prefer to keep the market unregulated, he argued.

"This shit is everywhere. The question is whether it is governed or not," Linton said. He added it was hard to ignore its great potential for job growth and scientific opportunity. Linton noted that there were great concerns about doctors not prescribing cannabis to patients, which led the industry to struggle. So, Canopy hired many drug experts from pharmaceutical companies, including Novartis and Pfizer, to educate doctors regarding cannabis. It helped Canopy vastly expand their business.

With Linton as Co-CEO of Canopy, the company grew quickly. His Co-CEO focused on operations while he focused on growth and outreach. He ascribed Canopy's success to the fact that it scaled well because of applied technology, extensive use of databases, Application Programming Interface (API), and software. He noted that it is relatively easy to be a global company if it is designed to scale. Linton added that Canopy's ability to deliver high-quality products in the nascent industry is what led it to stand out.

"When you're a tech nerd, you're good at not messing up," Linton said regarding his ability to deliver results. Canopy and its subsidiaries sell flowers, oils, concentrates, soft gel capsules, and hemp for both medical and recreational uses. One of its subsidiaries offers discounts to struggling medical patients.

At his height, Linton made deals with Snoop Dog and Martha Stewart to market their product lines under Canopy. Stewart got into cannabis after befriending Snoop Dog when they co-starred in a cooking show. Stories like Linton's are not likely to be isolated incidents as the industry changes, and larger, established companies test the waters. Many feel pharmaceuticals will follow Constellation's path, as will other alcohol manufacturers. Tobacco giant Altria Group already followed Constellation's path and invested $2.4 billion in the Canadian cannabis company Cronos.

The moral of the story might be that non-cannabis companies should moderate their expectations when plunging into deals with cannabis companies. Many companies seem thirsty for cannabis revenue without having experienced the difficulties of building a business around an illegal substance.

Because it is still illegal at the federal level, a host of problems remain. Problems with interstate commerce are a major issue in the industry. Companies cannot transport cannabis products across state lines. Thus, it is illegal to transport cannabis between two legalized states. Cannabis grown in one state must be sold in that state. That caused a crisis in Oregon where so much legal cannabis was grown that the price collapsed.[146] Many small businesses were adversely affected because there was such a surplus of cannabis that could not be sold elsewhere in the country. In 2015, there were only a few cannabis growers, and the price of cannabis was high.

There are other significant drawbacks to operating in the industry. For example, advertising is difficult due to restrictions on cannabis marketing. Many lawmakers oppose a cannabis company advertising itself with a cartoon mascot like Joe Camel. Like everything in cannabis, regulations around advertising vary state by state. For example, California allows billboard advertising while Colorado does not.

In terms of social media, Facebook has a strict prohibitionist policy regarding businesses related to cannabis, including hemp and CBD. It limits the ability to purchase Facebook ads, especially if the word "cannabis" is in your business name. Some companies have succeeded in buying Facebook ads, but most advise against doing so. Google and Twitter operate in a similar fashion.

Instagram is a friendlier environment, even if Facebook owns it since Instagram shuts down fewer accounts related to cannabis. However, people have still had their accounts shut down on both platforms. In an age of social media, that can severely hurt a company. Cannabis-related firms are often forced to rebuild their following from near scratch, which can be difficult. Many have resorted to making back up accounts for this very reason.

Furthermore, Multi-State Operators (MSOs) are often favored over small business entrepreneurs in the competition for licenses. It has become a serious issue in Missouri as well as in New Jersey. In Missouri, several MSOs and well-connected local companies received multiple licenses at the expense of entrepreneurs. Some say it is because the company given the contract to review license applications had conflicts of interest. Three hundred and thirty-eight licenses were awarded out of more than 2,266 applicants. One of the most serious issues is that different applications were granted a different amount of points for the same part of the application.[147] It made little sense. Thus, they sought to appeal the decision.

In 2015, Ohio voters defeated a cannabis ballot initiative that would have allowed a group in favor of legalization to set up a cartel whereby only a few businesses would have been able to profit from it.[148] It was so unpopular that cannabis advocacy groups, the Drug Policy Alliance, and the Marijuana Policy Project did not support it. Many progressive cannabis voters retain a suspicion of the larger cannabis companies.

Another issue with the industry is that as the global cannabis market matures, the industry is expected to consolidate with the MSOs buying up smaller ones, for better or worse. It will lead to many of the smaller operations built by long-time cannabis activists and entrepreneurs being bought out or run out of business in the worst-case scenario. The same thing has happened in virtually every industry in the United States.

NORML is concerned with securing access to the market for small businesses, especially for black and brown entrepreneurs from the communities most harmed by the War on Drugs and keeping tax rates low.

Their Executive Director, Erik Altieri, said legalization is always a learning process. In many states, tax rates were set high with a low supply of cannabis made available. Because of this, "folks will still go to where they went all these years," Altieri said.

Altieri said it was an important thing to note just because retail sales are established; there is still a larger fight over the cannabis implementation. In many states, legalization led to nepotism and cronyism from big corporations that never cared about it before trying to make money off it.

"We need to make sure licensing is fair and favorable, that it includes boutique shops, growers," Altieri said. "Workers can't be second class citizens."

MSOs have their own issues. The MSO MedMen is a good example. Their stock, traded on the Canadian Stock Exchange, lost most of its value in 2019, and the company hemorrhaged money to the tune of nearly $80 million. It seems they expanded too quickly by opening new dispensaries and buying up companies. A lot of the MSOs did this for the sake of expansion and did not see immediate results. While they were expanding, MedMen released a commercial directed by filmmaker Spike Jonze. It was mercilessly parodied by South Park in a video released in February 2019 that received more likes on YouTube than the original. It openly criticized them for their desire for profit above all else.[149]

MedMen did so poorly they laid off a significant number of workers and shut down a factory in Illinois. Then they closed their stores in Arizona after they donated $200,000 to the campaign for full legalization in that state.[150]

To make matters worse, they were facing two lawsuits. The first was a nearly $20 million lawsuit related to the treatment of former senior-level executives. In the suit, major investors alleged the company spent money frivolously by lavishing unnecessary corporate perks on the CEO and the President that enriched them at the expense of the company and the shareholders.

The second was a class-action lawsuit that claims they treated their employees poorly by severely underpaying them and failing to keep accurate records.[151] The lawyer for the plaintiffs called it wage theft. If they lose the suit, it means more will have to be spent to cover the expenses, at a time when that is difficult.

The MSO iAnthus has also had a whole host of problems. The company faced many issues after defaulting on a large loan, which led to an investigation that caused their CEO to resign. iAnthus came under great scrutiny when they were unable to make an interest payment of $4.4 million on their debt of $157.5 million to Gotham Green Partners. Founder and CEO Hadley Ford resigned from the company in April 2020 when the conclusion of the investigation was announced.

Investigators found he failed to disclose two loans that amounted to $160,000, which were deemed a conflict of interest. It was a conflict because they were personal loans to Ford. iAnthus underwent an internal investigation that included hiring Canaccord Genuity Corp. as a special advisor. They found that Ford should have disclosed the personal loans he received from a member of the board of Gotham Green Partners, which was attached to a larger loan to iAnthus. Ford was supposed to pay back the loan by March 31st and did not. In their announcement, the company said the investigation did not find that Ford's loan was directly tied to the company defaulting on the larger payment.

"Management and the board decided it was in the best interest of the Company and our stakeholders to spend our cash to maintain the inherent value of our business operations," said Ford said when the default was announced on March 31st, which smacked of impropriety.

Initially, the coronavirus pandemic was blamed for negatively impacting their business. The investigation raised a massive red flag, which led to Ford leaving the company under a dark cloud. Before founding iAnthus, Ford worked on Wall Street for 14 years.

Some shareholders were enraged at the default and were planning to sue the company. iAnthus was thought to be quite liquid in no danger of defaulting. The news of the default and investigation caused its stock price to fall. iAnthus is traded on the Canadian Securities Exchange, which halted trading of their stock two weeks ago to investigate the matter.

Gotham Green Partners is a major financial backer of the cannabis industry. Because it is difficult to secure bank loans since cannabis is still illegal on the federal level, it makes them especially powerful within the industry.

Ford's deputy Randy Maslow was appointed interim CEO. He was previously the company's president and a co-founder of iAnthus. Due to the tumult, iAnthus postponed releasing its 2019 fourth-quarter earnings report. Their scandal was not the first, nor will be it be the last scandal among the MSOs in the cannabis industry.

In June 2020, iAnthus announced that investment firm Gotham Green demanded repayment of the entire amount of a massive loan with interest, fees, costs, and other charges that have accrued, which amounted to about $160 million. Gotham Green invested in the company last year using a financial instrument known as a "Secured Debenture."

Because iAnthus did not file their records in time with the proper authorities, they cannot be traded on the Exchange. When their paperwork is filed for Fiscal Year 2019, they may be allowed to trade again. They traded at 30 cents a share in June 2020.

iAnthus likely failed to file their paperwork due to issues stemming from Gotham Green. They initially received an extension to file their paperwork due to COVID-19 and still could not make the deadline. The paperwork was due in early April 2020. It is possible they were seeking to hide significant losses.

iAnthus initiated a review process and hired Canaccord Genuity Corp. as its financial advisor. Their special committee of the board of directors reviewed a range of alternatives. According to a press release from iAnthus, Canaccord received several expressions of interest which, if completed, would repay the Secured Debentures in full and in cash. iAnthus owns and operates 35 licensed cannabis cultivation, processing, and dispensary facilities in 11 states.

The MSO Curaleaf, which operates a medical dispensary in Bellmawr, New Jersey, was severely fined in February 2020 by the Office of Safety and Health Administration (OSHA) for workplace violations.[152] OSHA initially fined them $40,000, but that was later reduced to $26,300. They were found to have seven workplace violations, including failure to have an eye rinse station and failing to provide electrical safeguards for their machinery, among others. On OSHA's website, all were listed as "serious violations."

The New Jersey Department of Health (DOH) investigated the violations as well. According to Commissioner Jeff Brown, the DOH was unaware of the violations before the story on Curaleaf's fines came out in *Politico*. When asked about further detail, Brown said he could not comment on the investigation and that "We're going to look into it. As the state regulator, we have a duty to do so."

Curaleaf is one of the largest dispensaries in New Jersey. They provided flower to GTI's Paterson dispensary until their cannabis can be harvested and sold. Curaleaf has similar deals with Harmony dispensary in Secaucus, NJ, and Garden State Dispensary's satellite location in Union Township, NJ, to provide cannabis. They have a contract to open three more facilities in New Jersey. Curaleaf was first found to have violated OSHA standards in July 2019. The company operates dispensaries in ten states.

MassRoots exemplifies issues the industry is facing. They rose to the top of the cannabis industry, at one point having sufficient capital to be part of a group of investors led by the firm, Oreva Capital, that purchased 60 percent of the legendary cannabis magazine *High Times*.[153]

Having gone public in 2016, MassRoots trades on the OTC market as MSRT. The price only ever ranged from about 25 cents to $2. The company has since seen its stock prices plummet to being worth less than one cent.[154] A great deal of fraud has been detected in penny stock trading.

The Securities Exchange Commission (SEC) took action against a group of MassRoots investors, including Douglas Leighton, David Hall, Michael Sullivan, Zachary Harvey, Paul Dutra, Jason Harmon, Jessica Geran, Bass Point Capital, and Azure Capital Corp. Led by Leighton, they were accused of manipulating the price of the stock in a traditional penny stock scheme of "pump and dump" whereby the price of the stock is artificially inflated by buying large quantities of shares to simulate active trading and then sold.

Leighton paid $1.5 million to settle the matter. He was also barred from the securities industry, holding office at a publicly-traded company, and from trading penny stocks.[155] According to the SEC, Leighton began the scheme before the company went public. The SEC did not accuse CEO Isaac Dietrich of being involved.

Chicago investor John M. Fife, the Managing Partner of Chicago Venture Funds, owns stock in MassRoots through three different companies. Fife has had his run-ins with the SEC, which alleged he engaged in a fraudulent scheme manipulating an insurance company.[156]

In 2016, MassRoots formed a partnership with the Canadian-based company Aphria to promote it on their social media platform. Aphria replaced most of its C-suite executives in March 2019 due to the fraudulent purchase of shell companies in Latin America.[157] Many of Aphria's investors, including Andy De Francesco, Barry Honig, John Stetson, and John O'Rourke, also invested in MassRoots.[158]

Honig paid $27 million to settle an SEC investigation that accused him of manipulating the market price of Riot Blockchain that O'Rourke ran as CEO.[159] The SEC also investigated Mark Grossman, who invested in Riot and MassRoots. They alleged that stock in Riot was acquired at a low price and then artificially inflated before being sold.[160] De Francesco's wife, Catherine, held the same voting power as O'Rourke, Grossman, and Stetson in MassRoots. She also owned a substantial amount of Riot shares.[161]

Dietrich was defensive about MassRoots' relationship with Aphria. He said that while DeFrancesco's company had invested nearly six figures, and he was grateful for their support, they were not involved in the company's operations.

"We accept capital from anyone willing to help and comply with regulations," Dietrich said. "That's a handful of investors out of 35,000." He said that Aphria's investment in MassRoots was wholly in compliance with the law.

He said he has no relationship with those under investigation. "They have nothing to do with MassRoots," he insisted.

Dietrich has been in a tenuous position within the company since 2017. He was briefly ousted, but, in a turn of events, most of the hostile board was ultimately ousted instead. Dietrich launched MassRoots in 2013 as a social media platform to serve as a community for cannabis lovers. He had little formal education and business experience at the time. Nonetheless, Dietrich launched the company at a young age with a few friends who have since left the company.

Aside from issues stemming from investors, the company has struggled with finding a profitable business model, having pivoted from being a social media company to a dispensary finder, a blockchain company, a cannabis rewards company, and then a cannabis logistics and supply chain company with the acquisition of COWA Science Corporation in 2019.

MassRoots desperately needed that revenue from COWA. The company has failed after multiple injections of capital to turn a profit. It burned through multiple rounds of capital from the largest investors in the cannabis industry, including Arcview, Poseidon Asset Management, and Dutchess Capital.[162]

MassRoot's initial social media presence, while fairly popular with 650,000 users at its height, generated useful data, but was never sufficiently monetized. However, Leafly and Weedmaps, competitors in the same space, successfully monetized their respective media platforms.

Poseidon has since divested its holding in MassRoots. The company declined to comment on its reasoning, calling such information regarding their relationship and investments into MassRoots "confidential for our L.P.s."

CHAPTER 17
SAFETY

Safety will become a lesser concern as the cannabis industry moves away from its underground past. People are comfortable buying legal cannabis products because they know what is going into their bodies due to proper labeling. With deaths in the fall of 2019 linked to vaping, consumers are looking for ways to use cannabis vaping devices safely. It was confirmed that people became ill because they used counterfeit vape cartridges in their vape pens.[163]

Initially, it was unclear what was causing people to get sick. Politicians jumped to the conclusion of banning cannabis vaping devices in the legalized markets. Because vapes do not produce clouds with the distinctive cannabis odor, their use is usually undetected. They also look like nicotine vaping devices. Thus, like bootleg movies, counterfeit cartridges flooded the market. Some politicians found it an appropriate time to attack tobacco vapes as well.

"These unfortunate incidents reinforce the need for greater regulation, standardization, and oversight of the cannabis market, principles which NORML has consistently called for in the cannabis space. Consumers must be aware that not all products are created equal," NORML's Deputy Director Paul Armentano said. "Quality control testing is critical and only exists in a legally regulated marketplace."

Professionals within the industry have known about the issues with counterfeits for a while. Oleg MaryAces, Director of Education for

Lock and Key Remedies, which sells cannabis vapes, oils, and topicals, explained that individuals have died, and many are in the hospital because they used counterfeit THC cartridges. These cartridges add an excessive amount of Vitamin E to the oil so that air bubbles move slower. The product thereby merely looks more potent.

"It's the tip of the iceberg," he said regarding the vaping industry's issues. According to MaryAces, along with Vitamin E, counterfeit cartridges might contain an excess of mold, heavy metals, and pesticides. MaryAces said his company spent a great deal of time ensuring their cartridges did not contain harmful chemicals such as pesticides, micro bacteria, or mercury. However, he said many in the industry were not previously interested in such issues.

"It's a big, big mess there," he said. Many counterfeit cartridges that look like those of respected brands are being manufactured in China and subsequently marketed on Instagram. Black market cartridges are often filled with questionable chemicals along with cannabis oil before being sold. It is especially distressing to companies seeking to produce safe cartridges.

For Armentano, none of the products sold on the black market are sufficiently safe. He compared it to other situations where one might find shoddy products on the black market. Unfortunately, illegal cartridges with a lethal amount of Vitamin E looked nearly identical to those sold by legal retailers. Because these companies are underground, they do not comply with regulations. In California, the underground black market is more than twice the size of the legal market.

"This is no different than any other market. If one buys a handbag from an unlicensed street vendor in New York City and the tag says 'Gucci,' chances are that it isn't. But if one buys a handbag from a licensed, brick-and-mortar brand name retailer and that bag says 'Gucci,' it most likely is," said Armentano.

Because cannabis is federally prohibited, even the legal market is not regulated by the FDA (Food and Drug Administration).

Armentano pointed out that the contents of most cannabis cartridges are largely unknown. He added that existing state regulations are inadequate and have not required testing for chemicals found in counterfeits.

"Products sold at licensed cannabis retailers in legal states that are manufactured by state-licensed entities, that are compliant with existing regulations, and that are lab-tested for purity before the market are likely going to be of greater quality and safety than those that are not," said Armentano. He explained that if cannabis were federally legal and acceptable, the FDA and other federal regulatory agencies would certainly have addressed tainted products.

MaryAces echoed Armentano's view saying, "If you regulated it, we wouldn't be having these deaths," he said.

Steps have since been taken to ensure the cannabis market is as safe as possible. The California Bureau of Cannabis Control (CBCC) mandated that cannabis retailers and delivery services have a Quick Response (Q.R.) code certificate on their windows in plain sight and a copy in their delivery vehicles.[164] That took effect immediately to address the vaping crisis. The regulatory change was pursued by the CBCC to allow consumers and law enforcement officials to be able to quickly discern the origin of a product and ensure its safety after the code is scanned. Q.R. codes will help consumers know they are purchasing a product from a vendor in the legal market.

The code certificate needs to be posted within three feet of any public entrance to a cannabis dispensary or "in a locked display case mounted on the outside wall of the premises."[165] In addition to paper, the Q.R. code certificate can be printed on glass, metal, or other material. It needs to be 8 ½ inches by 11 inches, the size of a standard sheet of paper. The code itself needs to be 3.75 inches by 3.75 inches.

The cartridges that caused the illnesses that led to the vaping crisis in 2019 originated in the underground market. Terra Carver of the Humboldt County Growers Alliance said it's "literally" a matter of "life or death" for consumers who are "trying to figure out if the dispensary they are shopping at is selling poisoned products or not."

In November 2019, the California Department of Public Health (CDPH) reported there were 163 cases of pulmonary disease-related to cannabis and e-cigarette vaping. According to the Center for Disease Control (CDC), there were 2,172 cases nationwide and 42 deaths.

"The proposed regulations will help consumers avoid purchasing cannabis goods from unlicensed businesses by providing a simple way to confirm licensure immediately before entering the premises or receiving a delivery," said California Bureau of Cannabis Control Chief Lori Ajax.

Those with smartphones in California can now scan the Q.R. codes to ensure a product comes from a licensed retailer. When a consumer scans the code, it will be sent to the BCC's License Search database. Once there, they will be able to see the business' license number, license type, its official name, contact information, business structure, premise address, license status, issue date, expiration date, and activities.

In addition, you can see whether the business holds a license for adult use, medical, or both. The database also includes phone numbers and email addresses for all cannabis businesses in the state and holders of multiple licenses, as well as links to respective websites. Active licenses are listed along with those that are suspended, canceled, revoked, inactive, or expired. California was the first state to initiate such a standard. Q.R. Codes will be effective for retailers who seek to promote their products as being especially safe.

The international cannabis vape pen supply chain was adversely affected by the outbreak of coronavirus, as was daily life in the legal cannabis hub of Seattle in March 2020, before it spread throughout the country. Cannabis vape batteries and pens are largely manufactured in China. Because of the outbreak, factories in China were not operating at their full capacity. Around 30 million vape pens and cartridges were previously arriving in the United States from China every month. Thus, the international supply chain has been disrupted. It negatively affected the vape pen industry, which was hurt by the Vitamin E scandal in 2019.

"A supply pinch is coming in weeks and will persist for months," said CEO of American Made Vapes, Dan Fung. "Prices will rise. Shortages of packaging and vape pens could occur." The pandemic began in China.

Along with manufacturing issues, the coronavirus pandemic devastated the world and the cannabis industry. One of the first places to be affected by the coronavirus was the legal city of Seattle, Washington, where 19 deaths had been reported by March 19, 2020.[166]

The South by Southwest (SXSW) conference, along with all other significant gatherings, were canceled shortly afterward. Several cannabis-related panels were planned for SXSW, which combines music, film, and business into one gigantic festival.[167] Cannabis industry leader Steve DeAngelo was among those slated to speak.

The overall supply of cannabis products was not greatly affected because they must all be grown, processed, and sold in the same state. But demand did become high, which caused dispensaries to run out of products. On the other hand, dispensaries that experienced increased sales began offering discounts to customers. Event organizers across the country who had elaborate plans for 4/20 had to reconsider them.

For cannabis users, the circle or "scythe" of consumers is the most common and communal manner to ingest it. While the scythe usually does not lead to illness, it was advised it should be avoided since the lethal illness could infect one if this were practiced. Unfortunately, while it has many great uses, it has yet to be proven that cannabis or CBD can help treat coronavirus.

Another negative consequence of the coronavirus pandemic was the death of Charlotte Figi. She was a medical marijuana patient who inspired and galvanized the cannabis industry. Charlotte passed at the age of 13 from coronavirus. Figi was born with Dravet Syndrome, which caused severe seizures. At the age of five, her parents began treating them successfully with CBD after Colorado legalized medical marijuana (or clinical cannabis). Her mother, Paige, called her recovery nearly miraculous.

"Charlotte slept soundly for the first time in years. She went seven days without a seizure. Over time, the seizures dropped from thousands a month to just a few. After not speaking for six months, she started talking again," Paige said after Charlotte began taking CBD.

At its worse, she had nearly 300 seizures a week. In addition to being unable to speak, Charlotte could not walk nor eat without a feeding tube by the time she started consuming medical marijuana. She had been on a feeding tube for two years by that point. Her family relocated to Colorado to take advantage of the change in medical marijuana laws. Charlotte's recovery caused her family to become ardent advocates for medical marijuana across the country.

Dr. Sanjay Gupta featured Charlotte on a CNN special that highlighted her recovery due to medical marijuana.[168] Filmed after she had been on clinical cannabis for about a year, she appeared to be a normal child. The CBD-heavy strain of cannabis, Charlotte's Web, was named after her. The Stanley Brothers created it in their Colorado Springs-based medical dispensary. Charlotte's Web helped Charlotte improve dramatically. The strain has such a low amount of THC you cannot get high from consuming it. She consumed the strain as an oil. The Stanley Brothers helped the Figis obtain it at an affordable rate.

Before her death, Charlotte had been sick for weeks. An initial test for CO-VID-19 turned up negative. Due to coronavirus, she had a seizure that caused respiratory failure and a heart attack. Dravet Syndrome likely left her vulnerable to the virus. Her death made national news.

"She grew, cultivated by a community, protected by love,

demanding that the world witness her suffering so that they might find a solution. She rose every day, awakening others with her courage, and with that smile that infected your spirit at the cellular level," the Stanley Brothers' website said about Charlotte. Before Figi became known for using it, the strain had not been popular

CHAPTER 18

THE UNDERGROUND MARKET

The Emerald Triangle, located north of San Francisco and consisting of Humboldt, Mendocino, and Trinity Counties, has been the center of outdoor cannabis growing in the United States since the 1960s.[169] It has welcomed thousands into its hills who, after spending time there, opened a business in the industry elsewhere. Conditions are said to be ideal for growing cannabis in the Emerald Triangle. The ideal conditions have made the area a mecca of cultivation. It has been compared to the cultivation of grapes for making wine in nearby Napa Valley. Many growers in the Emerald Triangle take pride in raising their cannabis organically without chemicals. As cannabis has become legal, growers in the Emerald Triangle seek to create craft cannabis products in the manner that fine wine is made.

Certain growers have only slowly adapted to legalization and the compliance with regulations and associated paperwork. Larger, better-funded operations can manage the red tape easier than smaller, independent growers who survived DEA raids.

Most underground black-market cannabis businesses operate in a less costly manner than that of the legal businesses. These underground pillars are not being warmly received by those who came into cannabis from legitimate industries. By the same token, they often look warily at the corporate entities which seem to seek to corner the legal cannabis market.

The Battle of Trenton: State vs. NJWeedman

As cannabis becomes legal, minorities are being excluded from the upper echelons of the industry and getting arrested for possession and distribution. One man is refusing to abide by the state's regulations and is daring authorities to arrest him. Ed "NJWeedman" Forchion (pronounced "for-shown") has become a controversial figure in New Jersey amidst the delayed passage of adult-use cannabis reform.

Forchion has been selling cannabis for years in New Jersey and feels both the current federal prohibition and the legalization bill that failed in 2019 are unjust. He believes the bill was discriminatory because it excluded felons, such as himself, from applying for a license to sell legally. Considering his leadership in the legalization movement as well as his experience in the industry in New Jersey and California, it seems particularly unjust.

Forchion is an adherent of the view espoused by Michelle Alexander in her book *The New Jim Crow*. She argued that America's criminal justice system makes second class citizens out of felons, the majority of whom are African American and Hispanic. Many benefits that are key to climbing the economic ladder are often denied to felons. Thus, in many ways, the situation resembles the old Jim Crow segregationist system. Forchion agrees with her acknowledgment that as cannabis is becoming legal, white men are reaping the benefits the most. Those who were previously imprisoned for selling cannabis will be excluded and continued to be jailed for not complying with the legal market regime. According to Erik Altieri of NORML, 600,000 people are arrested for cannabis possession every year in the United States.

According to the American Civil Liberties Union (ACLU), cannabis use is roughly equal among all racial groups. However, African Americans and Hispanics are four times as likely to be arrested for possession, and eight times more likely to be charged with possession with intent to distribute.[170]

In states that passed adult-use cannabis reform, there has been a great delay in addressing the expungement of the records of those harmed by the War on Drugs. Colorado was the first state to legalize in 2012 and passed a law in 2017 that allows those with misdemeanor use or possession convictions "to ask to seal, but not erase, criminal records if it is not currently a crime."[171] In California, when legalization passed in 2016, expungement was allowed, but no mechanism to implement it was outlined. Thus, cities and counties have taken a piecemeal approach. Many places are only erasing the records of those with simple possession charges and not trafficking. New Jersey is seeking to set up a similar mechanism.

In Forchion's view, Senator Nick Scutari (D-Union) wrote the bill S.2703, "The New Jersey Marijuana Legalization Act," to enable wealthy individuals to profit the most. The fact that companies seeking to sell cannabis were required to have about $2 million in the bank, in the 2019 round of medical marijuana license competition, justified Forchion's view.

"I built grow rooms and a dispensary in L.A. for far less," he added. Forchion is fed up with the way business is being done.

"There are dispensaries in New Jersey. Those are rich white corporations, Caucasian Cannabis Corporations (CCCs). New Jersey's pending legalization bill would have done the same thing. It would then be a couple hundred white guys selling weed, while we'd be expected to stop selling weed and patronize the CCCs or risk imprisonment," Forchion said. Thus, he invented the hashtag #sellingweedlikeimwhite to protest, as he openly sells cannabis while demanding to be included in legalization.

In September 2018, he went to the New Jersey Statehouse and announced to the Assembly that he was "selling weed like I'm white."[172] In March 2019, he sent letters to New Jersey's Attorney General Gurbir Grewal, and Craig Carpenito, the U.S. Attorney for New Jersey. He declared he "was selling weed like he's white," which he posted on his website and mailed to numerous media outlets. He argued that the dispensaries in New Jersey are just as much in defiance of the federal prohibition as he is. Still, because their owners are white, they are protected by New Jersey's medical marijuana law and the Compassionate Use of Medical Marijuana Act (CUMMA), while he is not.

His most public action occurred in November 2018 when he staged a protest in which he dressed in a prisoner's orange jumpsuit labeled "political prisoner 420" and stood outside New Jersey Governor Phil Murphy's office, openly selling small amounts of cannabis and plants.[173] (It was ironic he was selling plants. Even the legislators who support passing adult-use reform oppose "homegrow.") State police did not arrest him as he tried to light a joint, but merely told him to go to the area where the permit for the protest was granted.

"I've been selling weed like a white guy since," he said. Thus, for over a year, New Jersey has not arrested him but rather ignored him.

Since his last acquittal in May 2018, he dared Mercer County assistant prosecutor Stephanie Katz to prosecute him. Instead, pending charges were dismissed. He has been encouraging others to join him.

"There should be more people like me. If there's a thousand like me, then they can't ignore it," he said. "As you can see, it's easy to ignore a one-man gang like me; for over a year now, the state has looked the other way as I sell weed like the CCC owners in this state. I am the only black-owned dispensary in New Jersey, limited only by my illegality in state law. I should be as protected from the feds as the six white guys are. This is what I'm seeking from a jury of my peers, a public trial, but I'm being thwarted because Mercer County Prosecutor Stephanie Katz is ignoring me."

Forchion has been arrested numerous times. In 2000, when he was arrested for a series of weed distribution charges, he took a plea. He was initially facing 30 years but received ten years and only served seventeen months. When arrested, he discovered the concept of jury nullification, whereby the twelve members of a jury can decide that an individual is not guilty if they believe the law is unjust. He is a proud proponent of this tactic, which has served him well. Forchion points to the state Constitution, which says that "the truth may be given in evidence to the jury; and if it shall appear to the jury that the matter charged as libelous is true and was published with good motives and for justifiable ends, the party shall be acquitted; and the jury shall have the right to determine the law and the fact."

Thus, he seeks to "put the law on trial with a jury of my peers." Forchion said, "The people are the final arbitrators of the laws passed by politicians."

After winning more than one trial with jury nullification, Forchion is especially bold in his proclamations. He looks forward to going to court again.

"They know I'm the unconvictable Robin Hood of Reefer," Forchion said. "I don't think the state can get twelve (jurors) (#NJcantget12)." His point is that prosecutors cannot convince the standard 12 members of a jury to convict him unanimously. If there is one dissenter among the 12, the prosecution loses.

"That would be part of my opening statement: 'I'm being prosecuted for selling weed while not white and putting the law on trial,'" he added. "My public message to the authorities is: You can't convict! Go ahead! Arrest me! Let me be the martyr! I'm not taking a plea."

Pleading "not guilty" and fighting charges is not easy. The whole justice system is designed for expediency, with the expectation that you will take a "guilty" plea for the lesser consequences and not jam up the system with a trial. A significant part of the issue is the cost involved with fighting any charge, along with the fear of jail time.

In addition to his #SELLWEEDLIKEIMWHITE protest, Forchion ran for State Assembly in New Jersey's 15th Legislative District in the 2019 Assembly election on the Legalize Marijuana Party ticket. Towards that end, he passed out flyers and sold bags of flower to anyone interested while campaigning.

While he might seem like a radical, Forchion often espouses a simple belief in a free market system. He currently runs a café called NJWeedman's Joint, which adjoins his Liberty Bell Temple III. Due to its exemption as a religious organization, the Temple allows members who pay a small fee to smoke there without fear of repercussion. The café and Temple are across the street from Trenton City Hall. Unfortunately, the business has been slow, as city workers have been discouraged from patronizing his business.

Forchion previously ran a medical marijuana (or clinical cannabis) business known as Liberty Bell Temple II in Los Angeles until the Drug Enforcement Agency (DEA) shut it down in 2012.

"Out of 800, they went after me," Forchion said. He attributed it to his loud criticism of national cannabis laws.

Afterward, he returned to New Jersey, where he began selling in the underground market, which he had been doing before going to California. Forchion likens himself to General Douglas MacArthur in the Pacific theater in World War II.

"He was chased off by the Japanese, but he vowed to come back and fight. And he did, the American army and marines recaptured the Philippines. I feel the same way. I left Jersey in 2007. I hauled ass for a few years and in '13 came back to fight for all of us, for inclusion and I think I'm going to win," Forchion said. "The state will either have to deal with me or ignore me, but I'm not going away."

The underground market creates other issues besides a lack of anticipated tax revenue and a lack of social justice. Illegal growing operations sometimes disrupt protected wilderness areas. According to researchers with the United States Department of Agriculture's (USDA) Forest Service, the number of illegal marijuana crops grown in federally protected parks drops once a state legalizes cannabis.

"[W]e find that recreational cannabis legalization is associated with decreased reports of illegal grow operations on national forests," the researchers concluded. USDA Forest Researchers first analyzed U.S. Department of Justice data on the number of illegal grow sites between 2004 and 2016, alongside changes in state cannabis laws. Then they used their dataset to run simulations, comparing how different cannabis policies may influence the presence of illegal grows. They also used simulations to test the effects of marijuana tax laws and increased police enforcement on illegal grow sites.

Published in the journal *Ecological Economics*, the study found that "policies legalizing recreational cannabis production and consumption are associated with significantly lower numbers of reported illegal grows in national forests."[174]

Decriminalization alone did not have a curbing effect on illegal growing operations, which is logical since it does not allow for a system of legal cultivation or distribution. According to the simulations, a 20 percent increase in law enforcement manpower would spur only a 2.5 percent decrease in reported illegal grows.

Illegal cultivation would decrease with a 6 to 13 percent reduction in taxes on legal marijuana sales. However, the "availability of legal cannabis does not encourage illegal cultivation unless the after-tax price for legal cannabis is substantially elevated relative to the illegal product," the researchers wrote.

The researchers say the predictive models indicate that illegal marijuana grow sites would decline 35 to 51 percent across the United States if all states with medical marijuana legalized recreational use. Medical marijuana legalization alone appears not to have any impact on illegal grow operations.

"Arguably, our models hint that outright, national recreational cannabis legalization would be one means by which illegal growing on national forests could be made to disappear," the researchers concluded.

Environmentalists are particularly opposed to illegal marijuana growing because it often involves the use of harmful chemical fertilizers and pesticides that adversely affect the surrounding plant life.

Additionally, there are concerns over the uncontrolled use of clear-cutting and terracing of national parkland. That leads to a loss of trees and overall harm to places where nature is supposed to be protected.

CHAPTER 19
SOCIAL JUSTICE

The elusive nature of justice for the minority communities that have been most affected by the War on Drugs is a recurring theme throughout the legalization debate. Many participants are angry that while the underground market has a lot of successful minority entrepreneurs, the legal market has not developed similarly. Thus, a coalition made up of ten leading criminal justice and civil rights groups was formed to advocate that comprehensive social justice reform be included within federal cannabis legalization. Because cannabis legalization is on the radar of federal lawmakers, the Marijuana Justice Coalition (MJC) wants to ensure that those adversely affected by federal cannabis prohibition are not forgotten as a new profitable industry is established.

"As Congress considers the end of marijuana prohibition, the Marijuana Justice Coalition believes that any legislation that moves forward in Congress should be comprehensive," the MJC wrote. The groups that joined the MJC include:

- The American Civil Liberties Union (ACLU)
- Drug Policy Alliance (DPA)
- NORML
- Students for Sensible Drug Policy (SSDP)
- Center for American Progress (CAP)

- Center for Law and Social Policy (CLASP)
- Human Rights Watch[175]
- Immigrant Legal Resource Center
- Lawyers' Committee for Civil Rights Under Law
- Leadership Conference on Civil & Human Rights

The goals of the MJC include descheduling cannabis under the Controlled Substances Act, expunging the records of those with past cannabis-related convictions, and permitting individuals with felony convictions to participate in the industry. They also want to ensure that working in the industry does not adversely impact immigrants who are applying for citizenship.

The coalition aims to remove any penalties related to past cannabis use or previous convictions for those seeking access to public benefits, nutritional assistance, and public housing. As part of that initiative, the MJC calls for the elimination of drug test results as justification for not granting benefits to potential recipients or for separating children from families during custody cases. It would help those with felony cannabis convictions who have difficulty securing employment. The MJC has proposed that revenue derived from future taxes on legalized marijuana be invested in impoverished communities negatively impacted by the War on Drugs.

"Since the scheduling of marijuana as a controlled substance in 1970, over twenty million Americans have been unjustly arrested or incarcerated," said Justin Strekal, political director of NORML. "Entire communities have lost generations of citizens to cyclical poverty and incarceration that resulted from the collateral consequences of having a cannabis-related conviction on their record."

The coalition also supports the use of sales tax generated from the legal cannabis market to help minority entrepreneurs as they establish themselves in the industry.

"Black and brown people have been traumatized by our racist marijuana laws, and, as the federal government embraces reform, our groups will make sure that any proposal will repair the damage done to those communities," said Queen Adesuyi, policy coordinator of the DPA.

The ACLU has been a leading advocate for marijuana reform for some time. The national organization previously worked with civil rights advocates to redress racial injustices by sending letters that criticize actions by the Drug Enforcement Agency (DEA) and call for substantial reform.

"As the lead law enforcement agency for drug enforcement at the national level, the DEA is emblematic of how the drug war has been a devastating failure," the coalition declared in a letter. Research done by the ACLU has shown that African Americans are arrested four times as much as white Americans, despite using cannabis at the same rate.[176] What's worse, in 2018, more people were arrested for cannabis than for violent crimes.[177]

The MORE Act

The Marijuana Opportunity Reinvestment and Expungement (MORE) Act introduced by House Judiciary Chairman Jerry Nadler (D-NY) would decriminalize cannabis by removing it from the Controlled Substances Act (CSA). It largely leaves the nuances of the cannabis markets to be determined on the state level. The bill would also provide funding for the expungement of criminal records of those with past marijuana convictions. It would then remove the ban on federal benefits such as public housing from those with possession charges. If passed, agencies could no longer penalize individuals when dealing with citizenship or similar benefit issues. For example, a serious cannabis conviction can jeopardize one's student loans, receiving federal housing benefits, and losing certain professional licenses.[178]

As previously noted, cannabis is currently a Schedule I drug, meaning it is supposed to have no medicinal value and a high potential for abuse. For context, cocaine and methamphetamine are Schedule II drugs.

According to the DEA, "Schedule I drugs, substances, or chemicals are defined as drugs with no currently accepted medical use and a high potential for abuse. Some examples of Schedule I drugs are: heroin, lysergic acid diethylamide (LSD), marijuana (cannabis), 3,4-methylenedioxymethamphetamine (ecstasy), methaqualone, and peyote."

"Schedule II drugs, substances, or chemicals are defined as drugs with a high potential for abuse, with use potentially leading to severe psychological or physical dependence. These drugs are also considered dangerous. Some examples of Schedule II drugs are: (Vicodin), cocaine, methamphetamine, methadone, hydromorphone (Dilaudid), meperidine (Demerol), oxycodone (OxyContin), fentanyl, Dexedrine, Adderall, and Ritalin."[179] Thus the DEA considers cocaine and methadone to be less harmful than cannabis with heroin being equally as bad.

"We back the most comprehensive bill that ends prohibitions and acknowledges decades of harm and over-policing," said Adesuyi. "We shouldn't leave people in jail while wealthy men continue to get rich off this."

One notable feature of the MORE Act is that it would impose a five percent sales tax on cannabis and cannabis-derived products to create the Opportunity Trust Fund. The revenue would provide loans and grants to communities that have been hardest hit by the War on Drugs. Currently, a marijuana conviction impacts a person's ability to get a legitimate job, secure a variety of benefits, including college grants and loans, and puts permanent residents and green cards holders at risk for deportation, among other issues.

"It's only right to see people protected in a world where marijuana is no longer criminalized," she said. Adesuyi noted the bill would not legalize cannabis in any given state, but rather, end prohibition on the federal level.

Along with Congressman Jerry Nadler (D-NY), who is sponsoring the bill in the House, there are 49 other cosponsors, including Congressman Matt Gaetz (R-FL). It is interesting to note that while Gaetz ardently defended Trump during the impeachment saga, he has worked with Democrats to move cannabis reform forward.

"It's past time to right this wrong nationwide and work to view marijuana use as an issue of personal choice and public health, not criminal behavior," Nadler said. "Racially motivated enforcement of marijuana laws has disproportionally impacted communities of color."

In the Senate, the MORE Act was sponsored by Senators Kamala Harris (D-Calif.), Elizabeth Warren (D-Mass.), and Cory Booker (D-N.J.). While industry advocates favored passing the SAFE Banking Act first to improve banking for cannabis businesses, they also seem to be in favor of the MORE Act. The National Cannabis Industry Association (NCIA) and the Cannabis Trade Federation, for example, have been supportive. The NCIA said that "We are very happy to see an increased emphasis on how to address the racially and economically disparate impact of our failed federal drug laws."

Adesuyi said the DPA, and their coalition, were not in favor of the passage of the SAFE Banking Act before the MORE Act because it did not address the communities affected by the War on Drugs.

"Oftentimes, when Congress addresses an issue, they take one bite of the apple, and that's it, so we're making sure that communities aren't left behind," she said. Adesuyi argued that the MORE Act would be more effective because it deschedules cannabis, which negates the issues related to banking. If cannabis were not classified as such an illegal drug, banks would not have such a problem having cannabis companies as clients.

"It's the best marijuana bill we've seen introduced yet," she added.

There are groups worried about the cost of a tax increase that could lead to a situation in California where the legal cannabis has had difficulty competing with its underground market counterpart in part due to the high tax imposed on it.

Due to partisan rancor, the STATES Act might seem a more viable solution. It is comparable to the MORE Act and was also introduced by Warren and Booker. Like the MORE ACT, the STATES Act leaves legalization to the states, hence its name. However, it does not contain the social justice components that would address the inequities created by the War on Drugs. While the STATES Act has more bipartisan co-sponsors, it does not seem any closer to passage than the MORE Act.[180]

"The STATES Act is clearly not close to what this country needs. It doesn't even deschedule," said Adesuyi. She argued that in addition to maintaining scheduling, it does not help address benefits, further research, or protect non-citizens but merely acknowledges states' rights. Adesuyi was optimistic regarding the MORE Act's passage and believed it would be passed by the end of 2020.

"Both marijuana reform and criminal justice reform are bipartisan. The Senate just passed the FIRST STEP Act, which resulted in thousands of people coming home, including those with serious drug offenses," she said. "So, it shouldn't be much of an uphill battle when it comes to marijuana."

The MORE Act passed the House Judiciary Committee by a 24 to 10 vote. While the vote was largely on partisan lines, two Republicans, Congressman Gaetz and Tom McClintock (R-CA), voted in favor of the bill, which is expected to address many of the injustices of the War on Drugs.

"These steps are long overdue. For far too long, we have treated marijuana as a criminal justice problem instead of a matter of personal choice and public health," said House Judiciary Chair Jerry Nadler (D-NY), a long-time champion of legalization. "Whatever one's views on the use of marijuana for recreational or medicinal purposes, arresting, prosecuting, and incarcerating users at the federal level is unwise and unjust."

Conservative Republicans critics claimed the bill needed more hearings, which is a common tactic to delay reform. While it is likely that the MORE Act could pass the Democratic-controlled House of Representatives, it is unlikely to pass the Republican-controlled Senate. Senate Majority Leader Mitch McConnell (R-KY), while being a great fan of the lucrative potential of hemp, stands firmly against cannabis.

However, if the Democrats were to regain the Presidency and the Senate in the 2020 election, it would be more likely that major cannabis reform would pass.

Expungement

Erasing past criminal records, once cannabis becomes legal, is another contentious issue. In the states where legalization passed by ballot initiative, expungement was not included. Pennsylvania Governor Tom Wolf and Lt. Governor John Fetterman (both Democrats) announced a reform process to expedite low-level marijuana possession pardons and urged people to apply.[181] Under Pennsylvania marijuana law, minor marijuana possession offenses are classified as a criminal misdemeanor, subject to a fine of $400, 30 days in jail, and a criminal record.

"We have people languishing in our prisons for having done something that wasn't violent, didn't really hurt anybody else, and what we've done is we're spending $40,000 a year to incarcerate them," Wolf said.

The announcement came after Wolf announced his support of legalizing recreational cannabis. According to a local CBS-affiliate station, the Governor started considering cannabis reform in December 2018. Attorney General Josh Shapiro (D) has also endorsed reform.[182]

Shapiro said that "continuing to criminalize adult personal marijuana use is a waste of limited law enforcement resources, it disproportionately impacts our minority communities, and it does not make us safer."

Fetterman spent 98 days visiting 67 counties in Pennsylvania, talking to citizens about cannabis, and found widespread support for legalization. He encouraged those with low-level convictions to apply for the program he is spearheading as head of the state's Board of Pardons. Fetterman's findings on his tour led to a report released in 2019 that endorsed full cannabis legalization. The report said there was "near-unanimous support for decriminalization and mass expungement of non-violent and small cannabis-related offenses."

The lieutenant governor found that bipartisan support for cannabis came from the belief that legal dispensaries would create good jobs. Many parts of Pennsylvania, such as Fetterman's hometown of Braddock, are in desperate need of a new industry. Wolf and Fetterman would like to see the legislature specifically pass decriminalization and adult-use reform.

Fetterman acknowledged the legislative process takes time, saying that "one thing we can do right now is alleviate the burden of small amount, non-violent convictions that scar the lives of otherwise productive citizens."

"They shouldn't continue to suffer with employment and housing issues because they were convicted of doing something that most Pennsylvanians don't even think should be illegal," he added.

Fetterman, the former Mayor of Braddock, has been especially conscious of the numerous negative effects of the War on Drugs. Despite the backing of Pennsylvania's governor and lieutenant governor, cannabis reform, bipartisan support for cannabis reform might be difficult to gather. In response to the Governor's call for legalization, Republican leaders came out against reform, saying,

"We are disappointed, and frustrated Governor Wolf would promote recreational use of a ... Schedule 1 narcotic. We do not believe easing regulations on illegal drugs is the right move in helping the thousands of Pennsylvanians who are battling drug addiction."[183]

Republicans control both chambers of the Pennsylvania General Assembly by narrow margins.

Police have been using cannabis prohibition as a justification for overreach for decades, which fed pent up anger. Protestors enraged about the death of George Floyd dominated national news for almost two weeks, beginning at the end of May 2020. Floyd died on May 25th when Minneapolis police officer Derek Chauvin crushed his neck by kneeling on him for eight minutes. Floyd was arrested because a convenience store said he used a counterfeit $20 bill and might have been drunk. He said multiple times, "I can't breathe."[184] Floyd was unarmed. Chauvin, along with the other three police officers on the scene, has since been fired. He has been arrested for murder. Chauvin had a history of police brutality incidents.

Because the cannabis industry is being built on a formally illegal product, the issue of Black Lives Matter (BLM) and the late George Floyd resonate. Cops have asserted their superiority in the name of "justice" for far too long, according to the many protestors.

How many lives were ruined by police, who saw too many cop action movies, trying to make a quota? Police brutality, hatred of cops, and their ego trips when dealing with the public led to the outrage, which was channeled into protests that broke windows. It all led to this.

A police van was burnt, and many were arrested at a Brooklyn protest near the Barclay's Center. The train stop at Parkside Ave., on the opposite corner of Prospect Park from the Barclays Center, in a predominantly Caribbean neighborhood, was flooded with people yelling for justice on Saturday, May 30, 2020. Five helicopters hovered over the neighborhood monitoring the situation. BLM signs were posted around the neighborhood the next day.

Across the country, many protesters were injured. The situation became so bad, tips for coping with tear gas were posted on Twitter. Chemicals can stay on one's hand and have adverse effects when touching sensitive body parts, even if not visible, according to one post. Police were injured according to news reports. How many protesters were injured before policemen were injured? On social media, people posted that they were attacked despite protesting peacefully. Many people erupted in anger over the situation. Social justice-minded organizations said they were "in solidarity" with the protesters and supporting them. The power of social media made George Floyd's death so well-known. If not for a phone camera, his death would have been another grim statistic in a world full of them.

A riot is what happens when people who feel beaten down do not know what else to do. It has been true throughout history from the Byzantine Empire to the aftermath of the death of Martin Luther King, to now. These are the times that make the history books. May George Floyd's death not have been in vain.

Cannabis Prisoners

One of the biggest issues in the cannabis controversy is that while the industry is thriving, many are still serving sentences for cannabis-related crimes for doing exactly what the legal corporations are doing. Former cannabis crime kingpin John Knock feels he should be released, not only because of the time he has served but to stop the spread of COVID-19 as well. Knock is serving two life sentences in a federal prison in Southern New Jersey. He ran an international cannabis smuggling empire importing marijuana and hash to the United States. Authorities estimated he was previously worth $200 million.[185]

Since 1996, Knock has been incarcerated for his cannabis crimes. He is now very sick, partly due to the inadequate healthcare he received in jail. Knock sought parole last fall based on his ill health. But he failed to convince the warden. The former perpetrator of cannabis crime is now 72 and has no history of violence. He has been a model inmate, even leading yoga classes for his fellow prisoners.

NORML leader and attorney David Holland is representing him.

Holland said Knock has the normal maladies of a 72-year old man. He has a particular nasal sinus infection and a swelling in his ankle that impedes his ability to walk. Holland said the case and argument release is "very unique, not based just on his health condition, but on the fact that society has changed its view on cannabis and done away with life sentences, like life in prison."

He also argued that bigger cannabis crime kingpins received far lighter sentences. The FIRST STEP Act signed by Trump in December 2018 got rid of life sentences without the possibility of parole after it was recognized to be excessive. In addition, a provision was added that seniors could also be released if they had served at least 10 years or 75 percent of their sentence. Holland argues that given the time Knock has served, he should be eligible for release.

"Cannabis law has changed, no longer are life sentences handed down, we're looking for some justice based on the changing attitudes of Congress," Holland said.

Knock was arrested in Paris in 1996 for cannabis crime operations. He was later extradited to the United States in 1999. It was agreed he would only serve 20 years based on an existing treaty between the United States and France. Knock also received a harsher sentence than the others for seeking to defend himself via a trial. In 2012, Holland was part of the legal team that succeeded in persuading the Obama Administration to grant clemency to four other prisoners in jail serving life sentences without parole, but not for Knock.

The U.S. Attorney's Office of Northern Florida has sought to deny Knock's release. They previously claimed the judge did not have the authority to release him. The federal judge they petitioned is based is in Gainesville, Florida, where the case was originally tried.

The inhumane practice of solitary confinement was severely restricted in New Jersey in 2019. Despite that, Knock sits in his cell alone nearly all day since this is the best way the prison has to cope with the pandemic. In prison, many people are naturally kept in close quarters, which makes social distancing impossible. Knock has made the best of it with many books to read, a radio on which he listens to NPR and snacks.

Knock's sister started a non-profit advocating for non-violent cannabis prisoners like her brother to be released. Many of the prisoners with whom she keeps in touch are in fear of being added to the long lists of anonymous COV-19 victims. There are likely many more cases like Knock's.

A great deal of talk took place regarding the release of sick prisoners to stop the spread of coronavirus. Still, few have been released since the announcement by Governor Phil Murphy in late April 2020.

CHAPTER 20

RUNNING ON CANNABIS

The increasing popularity of cannabis reform has induced more politicians to support it. Initially, the idea of being pro-cannabis after decades of prohibition and the War on Drugs seemed ludicrous. However, as time has passed, cannabis has become less threatening. The public has seen that cannabis certainly has medical benefits. Furthermore, there is the potential of creating a new government revenue stream worth millions of dollars without having to raise taxes. While this has occurred slowly but surely, the effects are being seen, which has led to politicians endorsing cannabis reform.

For example, in New Jersey, when he ran for Governor in 2017, Phil Murphy was open about his pro-cannabis stance. Murphy won a comfortable victory against Christie's Lieutenant Governor Kim Guadagno.[186]

During the 2018 New York Gubernatorial Democratic primary, Cynthia Nixon touted her position on cannabis legalization at the only scheduled primary debate. In response to her platform, the current Governor and Democratic primary rival, Andrew Cuomo, was forced to the left on the issue.

"I think it's very important that we legalize marijuana in New York State. Eight other states have done it, plus the District of Columbia," Nixon said during their debate. "There are a lot of reasons to do it, but first and foremost, because it's a racial justice issue. People across all ethnic and racial lines use marijuana at roughly the same rate, but the marijuana arrests are 80 percent black and Latino."

Nixon raised the issue of criminal justice reform when discussing cannabis in contrast to others who tout the benefits of marijuana legalization to the state's coffers.

She continued by saying, "We need to follow the Oakland model, we need to follow the Massachusetts model and prioritize those communities not only for licenses but for small-business loans and other supports. And we need to use the tens of millions of dollars that we will have in revenue to invest in those communities that have been targeted and pay for job training and pay for education programs. And we need to parole people who are in jail for marijuana arrests, and we need to expunge their records and use some of this tax revenue for them to reenter."[187]

While conceding the need to investigate legalization, at best, Cuomo moved cautiously on cannabis. He announced the formation of a workgroup to study the issue and put together a regulatory framework in Fall 2018. It was notable that he did not concur with Nixon on the need for criminal justice reform to reduce the damage done to communities as a result of the War on Drugs.

In contrast, Nixon consistently raised the issue, giving her campaign momentum. On April 20, 2018, Mary Louise Parker, the star of the hit TV show "Weeds," where she played a cannabis-dealing suburban mother, hosted a fundraiser for Nixon. Cuomo responded by rallying sufficient forces and won the primary.

As previously noted, Michigan's Governor Gretchen Whitmer and Attorney General Dana Nessel both supported cannabis reform when running in 2018 concurrently with the legalization referendum. In 2018, Illinois gubernatorial candidate J.B. Pritzker also ran on legalizing adult-use cannabis.[188] And true to his word, it passed within his first year in office.

Not every candidate who supports cannabis wins. The 2018 Democratic Gubernatorial nominees in Florida and Maryland both supported cannabis reform and lost. That is not to say they lost because of cannabis, though. Florida Democratic nominee Andrew Gillum came within a percentage point of winning but lost momentum when figures close to him were revealed to be under federal investigation and began pointing fingers.[189] In Maryland, the Republican Governor Larry Hogan has been supportive of certain cannabis reforms. Hogan has governed as a moderate, which garnered him the support of many swing voters in Maryland. More importantly, he outraised Democratic nominee Ben Jealous. Cannabis reform polls well in Maryland.[190]

As states legalize, politicians are changing their positions. Senator Cory Gardner (R-CO) was initially wholly against legalization. As the market has developed in Colorado since legalization, he has been vocal about letting states set their policy in favor of cannabis. Thus, legalization is gaining support from Members of Congress where legalization has passed.

"The wave is cresting here where politicians can't ignore the issue," Erik Altieri of NORML said.

Presidential Politics

Cannabis legalization became an issue in the 2020 Democratic presidential primary, with candidates honing their relevant policy positions to stand out from the pack. At a debate held in February 2020, the candidates touted their positions.[191] While in South Carolina during the race, Senator Bernie Sanders asked people a crowd to raise their hands if they had been arrested for cannabis possession. Many did so.

"Holy God, whoa. That's a lot of people," Sanders said about the number of hands.[192] Many told distressing stories about being arrested for small amounts of cannabis and the severe negative consequences that followed. Sanders endorsed cannabis legalization in his prior run for the Democratic nomination in 2015 and has maintained his position since.

"This isn't a recent conversion for Sanders either, as he called for drug policy reform for much of his career and made marijuana legalization a cornerstone of his criminal justice reform platform in both his 2016 and 2020 presidential campaigns," said Altieri. Sanders released a thorough criminal justice reform plan, to be enacted if he takes office, that included the legalization of recreational cannabis for adults, as well as assistance to those in recovery from heroin addiction.

He released his reform program in the summer of 2019 to much fanfare from his supporters. According to the plan, Sanders would order the Attorney General to declassify and remove cannabis from the Drug Scheduling System. Then he would push a bill through Congress to allow the states to legalize cannabis at their own pace. In addition, a system to expunge the records of felons would be set up. He would also remove felonies as barriers to employment and other relevant applications. Collected tax revenue would partially to minority entrepreneurs and businesses "that are at least 51% owned or controlled by those in disproportionately impacted areas or individuals who have been arrested for or convicted of marijuana offenses."

Sanders gained the support of many due to his stance on economic reform. But many were wary of him due to his status as a self-proclaimed Socialist and his previous lack of affiliation with the upper echelons of the Democratic Party, which he touted as a strength.

Sanders was not the only candidate to come out strongly in favor of full legalization. Most of the Democratic contenders did so. In contrast, former Vice President Joe Biden has a mixed background and stance on cannabis.[193] Many criminal justice reform advocates blame him for being the chief proponent of the 1994 crime bill, which, while linked to a significant drop in crime, also resulted in the arrest of many individuals for possession. Their subsequent felony records made it difficult for them to succeed financially.

"Joe Biden has no legalization plan and as such is far out of touch with not just Democratic primary voters, but the American public as a whole," said Altieri.

Biden has defended his past, citing the drop in crime as proof of the bill's validity in justifying his stance. As he campaigned for President for the third time, Biden remained opposed to the full legalization of adult-use recreational cannabis. Rather he is in favor of decriminalization, which allows possession of small amounts of cannabis but does not set up a legal market, nor does it bring in the tax revenue a legal industry does. His campaign website, as of May 2020, did not specify a specific amount that would be decriminalized.[194] It was merely included under several criminal justice reform proposals.

Biden also called for expungement throughout his campaign. He seeks to make cannabis a Schedule II drug, which would allow it to be prescribed legally. While Vice President, he was in favor of the Cole Memo, which stopped the federal government from disrupting state markets, and expressed a desire to end the War on Drugs. As a seasoned politician, Biden is not immune to persuasion on the merits of cannabis reform. When Obama and Biden first ran together in 2008, they were both publicly against gay marriage.[195] But, by 2012, Biden convinced Obama to support gay marriage. They both subsequently proclaimed their support of gay marriage in the re-election campaign to garner votes.

"Politicians are always lagging behind public opinion. They always wait for a parade and then run to get in front of it," Altieri said. Even a unified Democratic government is no guarantee. Legalization still needs grassroots pressure, no matter who controls Congress.

CHAPTER 21
THE FUTURE

While cannabis has had its dark days, its future looks bright. It is more a question of "how and when" than "if" full federal cannabis legalization will occur. Even with the market decline of some cannabis stocks, 2019 was a positive year for the legal industry. Formerly confined to the shadows and a few western states, cannabis and its derivatives have become big business across the country.

A sign of its mainstream, bipartisan acceptance is that former Speaker John Boehner (R-OH) joined the board of the cannabis MSO Acreage Holdings in spring 2019.[196] While in Congress, Boehner was never in favor of reform. In 2009 he said he was "unalterably opposed" to decriminalization. Boehner explained that as legalization has grown in support, his position has changed. He is also likely to profit from its expansion, along with others who support legalization.

In the same vein, former Los Angeles Mayor Antonio Villaraigosa joined the board of MedMen in August 2018. His record on marijuana while in office was mixed. While he initially prevented medical marijuana dispensaries from opening within Los Angeles, Villaraigosa supported the ballot initiative in 2016 that legalized the sale of marijuana to those 21 and older in California.

MedMen has close to ties to the former mayor. The company was one of the few in the cannabis industry that donated a large sum to Villaraigosa's failed gubernatorial bid. Gavin Newsom, the winner of the race, made a conscious effort to win the support of industry business owners. Villaraigosa, a Democrat, served two terms as mayor of Los Angeles from 2005 to 2013 and was the Speaker of the California State Assembly from 1998 to 2000. Villaraigosa was appointed by President Obama to chair the 2012 Democratic National Convention.

However, there is still the old stigma of "reefer madness" that is preventing the industry from growing to its full potential. By the same token, though, certain people will be disinclined to get into the industry while others can take advantage of that. Those who get into an industry early are those who are most likely to become leaders of it.

It is remarkable to think that the legal recreational cannabis industry is only six years old as of summer 2020, beginning with the opening of Denver's adult-use market on New Year's Day 2014.[197] It truly is in its infancy. Any industry in its first few years will attract companies scrambling for market share. The first few companies that initially seem big might become relics quickly. (When was the last time you played a game on an Atari?)

Medical marijuana first became legal in California in 1996, but throughout most of its early history, its purveyors were harassed by the federal government. Such harassment was not conducive to innovation and expansion. Since the Obama Administration, the markets have been more protected from the DEA's harassment.

Some say the next Democratic president will legalize cannabis. Apart from the presidency, the federal passage of bills requires both chambers. Thus far, the Republican-controlled Senate has not been inclined to pass any measure related to cannabis legalization. Therefore, it is most likely the Democrats will have to control both chambers of Congress and the presidency to pass significant cannabis legislation. It remains unclear if they can obtain a majority sufficient to overcome opposition.

Furthermore, given the amount of other important issues that need to be addressed, it will be difficult. That was the case during Barack

Obama's first two years. After passing the stimulus, the Affordable Care Act, and Dodd-Frank banking reform, there was not enough time to pass significant immigration, environmental, and transportation legislation before the Republicans took back the House in the midterm elections and blocked the proposed bills. Thus, those issues were largely unresolved by the end of the Obama Administration.

Due to the economic downturn caused by the global pandemic, many cannabis advocates sought aid for the industry after it was excluded from the CARES Act. Those in cannabis have been unable to access industry aid because cannabis is a Schedule I drug and illegal substance. Businesses that deal directly with cannabis production and sale, along with many ancillary service providers, are also ineligible for any SBA programs.

Many indirect businesses have not been declared essential and were forced to close. Cannabis businesses remained open, having been deemed essential. However, they had to cope with supply chain disruptions, excessive tax rates, and lack of access to banking services. They have also had to bear the costs incurred by implementing additional health and safety measures to protect employees and customers.

Legislation to give legal marijuana businesses, which have been declared essential, access to resources made available by COVID-19 response packages was introduced in the House by Rep. Earl Blumenauer (D-OR) and Ed Perlmutter (D-CO). The Emergency Cannabis Small Business Health and Safety Act would allow cannabis businesses, and those that provide services to them, to be included in those receiving industry aid provided through the Small Business Administration (SBA).

"The cannabis industry employs nearly a quarter of a million Americans and has been deemed essential in state after state, yet many businesses will not survive the pandemic without help," said Aaron Smith, executive director of the National Cannabis Industry

Association (NCIA). "They already face disproportionate financial burdens during normal conditions, and the strains created by the coronavirus response are putting them at an even greater disadvantage and jeopardizing their ability to provide vital healthcare services."

The NCIA is one of the largest cannabis business advocacy organizations. Together with industry advocates, the Cannabis Trade Federation, the Global Alliance for Cannabis Commerce, Minority Cannabis Business Association, and the National Cannabis Roundtable, they have been seeking industry aid for their respective members.

Congressman Blumenauer and nearly three dozen other Members of Congress sent a letter to House leadership urging them to make cannabis businesses eligible for SBA programs.

"Like other businesses with continued operations, cannabis businesses have met the moment by preserving access to treatment for patients with chronic conditions, donating protective clothing, and manufacturing equipment for medical use. However, unlike other small businesses, cannabis businesses are not eligible for the CARES Act programs," they said in the letter.

"State-legal cannabis businesses need access to CARES Act programs to ensure they have the financial capacity to undertake the public health and worker-focused measures experts are urging businesses to take," they added.

Senators Jacky Rosen (D-NV) and Ron Wyden (D-OR), along with eight co-signers, recently sent a similar letter to Senate leadership.[198]

Regardless of what happens on the federal level, efforts are underway to legalize cannabis across the country state by state. In New York, Connecticut, and New Mexico, lawmakers were seeking to pass adult-use cannabis reform through the legislative process.[199] Thus far, Illinois is the only state to pass full recreational cannabis legalization through traditional means. Every other state passed full legalization as a ballot measure. In New Mexico, Governor Michelle Lujan Grisham has been eager to pass the bill but has had difficulty swaying the New Mexico State Senate.

In Kentucky and Tennessee, lawmakers were seeking to pass a medical marijuana bill but had a great deal of difficulty doing so.[200] In Kentucky, medical marijuana reform legislation passed the House, but the State Senate Judiciary Chairman was an obstacle. Due to COVID-19, the Senate was forced to focus on other matters before it adjourned in April.[201] In Tennessee, an amendment was added to the bill that would not allow the program to take effect until cannabis is descheduled from being a Schedule I drug under the Controlled Substances Act.[202] Tennessee adjourned its legislative session early due to COVID-19.[203] Both measures were considered restrictive compared to others.

A few states have already established that cannabis reform will be on the 2020 November election ballot. For example, in New Jersey, there will be a referendum for adult-use legalization, and in South Dakota, there will be a referendum for medical marijuana. While legalization has been greatly delayed in New Jersey, they could still beat Pennsylvania and New York to the finish line.

Advocates in Arizona, Arkansas, North Dakota, Ohio, and Oklahoma were in the process of collecting signatures for adult-use cannabis referendums when this was published. Unfortunately, some ballot referendum efforts were halted because the outbreak of COVID-19 made it impossible to collect sufficient signatures in time.

Arizona failed to pass an adult-use measure in 2016 by only two percent. So, they want to try again in 2020. However, there were initially two different campaigns led by different interests.[204] One campaign was backed by the existing dispensaries, which are run by MSOs, while the other has support from ancillary businesses. Safe and Smart Arizona, the campaign backed by the MSOs, gathered enough signatures to qualify for a November referendum while the other suspended operations.[205]

In Idaho and Mississippi, legalization advocates were collecting signatures to pass medical reform when this book was published. Because these states are known for being especially conservative, it is very significant. Collecting enough signatures to qualify for a ballot referendum can be difficult. Due to measures taken to prevent the spread of coronavirus, some states allowed digital signatures rather than traditional physical signatures. In Florida, activists failed to collect enough in time for a 2020 recreational legalization campaign. Missouri advocates were prevented from gathering signatures due to the coronavirus, along with several other states.[206] Regardless of coronavirus, cannabis reform will continue to spread over the long-term, even if it takes longer than expected. For those measures that are on the ballot, it will be interesting to see how the drive to remove Trump from office affects the cannabis referendum and vice versa. In blue states, it is expected to help pass cannabis reform.

In addition to efforts to establish legalization, in Vermont, advocates sought to pass a law to create a market for the sale and taxation of cannabis, rather than its current strange gray situation whereby possession and growing cannabis is legal, but not the sale. The measure passed the Vermont State Senate in 2019, and the House in February 2020. A 20 percent tax on it was included to appeal to Vermont Governor Phil Scott (R), who wanted a portion of that revenue to goes toward after-school programs.[207] He also wanted to include a mechanism to test drivers' saliva to determine if they're impaired due to cannabis. The different versions will likely be reconciled and become law.

Even once a state legalizes cannabis, it takes time for dispensaries to begin selling legal cannabis. For example, a full two years elapsed between Massachusetts voters approving cannabis on the ballot and legal cannabis becoming available for purchase. The first dispensary in Boston, the largest city in Massachusetts, took even longer to open.[208] Illinois only took about seven months to open its adult-use market.

An issue among those who care about medical marijuana programs is that if clinical cannabis patients can get the same products from the legal adult-use market, the adult-use market will take a lot of patients away from the medical programs. Or if dispensaries can sell to both, they will cater more to the recreational consumers than the patients. If the budtenders can offer strains to help with different ailments, it would be more pleasant than going to a doctor and paying for check-ups to simply go the adult-use route.

If cannabis becomes fully legal under federal law, it is likely it could be sold in mainstream stores for a far more affordable price than the current range. It would also mean the system of cannabis dispensaries might disappear if cannabis were sold behind the counter of convenience stores, next to cigarettes. Brands might be sold in craft cannabis stores, depending on how legalization plays out. The cannabis industry could soon be comparable to the wine industry, with a few major companies dominating production and many craft, mom and pop brands making a name for themselves. As in many situations, more established and well-funded companies will be able to take advantage of the situation.

As previously noted, due to federal prohibition, the industry is barred from doing business over state lines. For example, a company growing in California cannot sell cannabis in Arizona. That would change, of course, once cannabis is legalized. The implications are far-reaching. A company that has spent a lot of money to grow cannabis indoors, in a state inhospitable to growing outdoors, is unlikely to continue to spend that money if it can buy or produce cannabis more cheaply in a state where outdoor growing conditions are ideal. Thus, the cannabis supply chain would increase from the state level to the national level, and eventually, the global level. This would radically change the cannabis industry. It also shows how, despite all the advances, we are still in the early stages of how far cannabis could go.

Overall, the future is bright as more states move toward legalization. Cannabis, hemp, and CBD all have great potential to make life better for millions of Americans in numerous ways for years to come.

"We have the American people at our back, and we'll finally see prohibition crumble and be a relic of history," Altieri said.

APPENDIX
HOW TO HELP

If you want to help the cause, you should join a group devoted to legalization. There is always strength in numbers. Advocates are always eager for more help! NORML is among the more established groups that advocate for cannabis legalization. The ACLU also does a great deal to support cannabis reform. There are local groups as well. If you are already a member of a civically-minded community organization, then getting the group to endorse cannabis reform can be especially helpful. Pro-cannabis coalitions are generally eager to have more groups on their side. It's especially helpful if you can persuade existing community leaders like local politicians, union leaders, faith leaders, and prominent businesspeople to endorse cannabis reform since their opinion carries weight in their respective communities.

Ballot initiatives always need help convincing voters. It includes going door to door persuading voters, collecting signatures at public events, making calls, and donating money, especially money.

For an advocacy campaign, write, call, and talk to your elected officials in person to persuade them to support legalization. Bringing friends and family with you helps as well to show popular support. While they are always hearing from lobbyists, it is different when constituents advocate for it. The more public support an issue has, the more likely the law will change.

ABOUT THE AUTHOR

D aniel L. Ulloa is an accomplished writer who covered politics and policy on all levels of government before focusing on cannabis. In cannabis, Ulloa has been covering progress on legalization, the industry's developments, and start-ups for a variety of publications. He is currently the Editor of Heady NJ, a local news site covering cannabis reform and the industry blooming as a result in New Jersey and the surrounding region. Ulloa is also Editor-in-Chief of CannaCulture.com and 420Studio.

In a volunteer capacity, Ulloa is Vice President of Communications for the Latino Action Network, which he represents on New Jersey's pro-cannabis ballot campaign NJ CAN 2020. He received a bachelor's degree in Political Science from Syracuse University and a master's degree in Legislative Affairs from George Washington University.

Endnotes

[1] The History of Cannabis Museum. (n.d.). The History. Retrieved from The History of Cannabis Museum: https://thcmuseum.org/the-history/

[2] Jane Marcus, Holy Cannabis: The Bible Tells Us So, Huffington Post, http://www.huffingtonpost.com/jane-marcus-phd/holy-cannabis-the-bible-t_b_4784309.html (last updated Apr. 16, 2014).

[3] Duvall, C. (2015). Cannabis. London: Reaktion Books .

[4] Mabillard, Amanda. *Did Marijuana Fuel Shakespeare's Genius? Shakespeare Online.* 20 Aug. 2000. (May 5, 2020) < http://www.shakespeare-online.com/biography/notedweed.html >.

[5] Marijuana Timeline. (2014). Retrieved from PBS: https://www.pbs.org/wgbh/pages/frontline/shows/dope/etc/cron.html

[6] Wren, C. S. (1999, April 1). U.S. Farmers Covet a Forbidden Crop. Retrieved from The New York Times: https://www.nytimes.com/1999/04/01/us/us-farmers-covet-a-forbidden-crop.html

[7] Hopper, T. (2019, February 6). Sorry, but George Washington and the Founding Fathers never actually got high. Retrieved from The Growth Op: https://www.thegrowthop.com/cannabis-news/sorry-but-george-washington-and-the-founding-fathers-never-actually-got-h

[8] The Use of Cannabis, Other Than as Hemp in Colonial

America. (2003). Retrieved from The Herb Museum: http://www.herbmuseum.ca/content/use-cannabis-other-hemp-colonial-america

[9] Sarah. (n.d.). Things You Must Know About Gender In Cannabis Plants. Retrieved from I Love Growing Marijuana by Robert Bergman: https://www.ilovegrowingmarijuana.com/things-must-know-gender-cannabis-plants/

[10] Halim, S. (2019, August 27). Dr Raphael Mechoulam and his revolutionary cannabis research. Retrieved from Health Europa: https://www.healtheuropa.eu/dr-raphael-mechoulam-revolutionary-cannabis-research/93049/

[11] Breathes, W. (2012, Novemeber 1). The history of cannabis in Colorado...or how the state went to pot. Retrieved from Westword: https://www.westword.com/news/the-history-of-cannabis-in-coloradoor-how-the-state-went-to-pot-511847

[12] Brown, B. (2019). Cannabis: The Illegalization of Weed in America. New York: First Second.

[13] Ibid.

[14] Smith, L. (2018, February 28). How a racist hate-monger masterminded America's War on Drugs. Retrieved from Timeline: https://timeline.com/harry-anslinger-racist-war-on-drugs-prison-industrial-complex-fb5cbc281

[15] Ibid.

[16] Re-criminalizing cannabis is worse than 1930s 'reefer madness'. (2018, January 18). Retrieved from The Conversation: https://theconversation.com/re-criminalizing-cannabis-is-worse-than-1930s-reefer-madness-89821

[17] Herer, J. (1985). The Emperor Has No Clothes. Austin: Ah Ha Publishing.

[18] PROCON.ORG supra note 3 (citing LaGuardia Committee

Report on Marihuana, THE MARIHUANA PROBLEM IN THE CITY OF NEW YORK (1944).

[19] (Department of Agriculture. Office of Public Affairs. (2015, July 26). Hemp for Victory. Retrieved from YouTube: https://www.youtube.com/watch?v=d3rolyiTPr0&list=WL&index=54&t=9s

[20] Dope & Glory: Reefer songs. (2002, November 5). Retrieved from All Music: https://www.allmusic.com/album/dope-glory-reefer-songs-mw0000663723

[21] Glass, L. (2015, May 7). The Mighty Mezz, Marijuana, and the Beat Generation. Retrieved from Los Angeles Review of Books: https://lareviewofbooks.org/article/the-mighty-mezz-marijuana-and-the-beat-generation/

[22] Meet the Waldos. (2019). Retrieved from 420Waldos: https://420waldos.com/

[23] McAlister, E. A. (n.d.). Encyclopedia Britannica. Retrieved from Rastafari: https://www.britannica.com/topic/Rastafari

[24] Schulze, E. (2018, September 20). Why Amsterdam is jealous of America's growing weed industry. Retrieved from CNBC: https://www.cnbc.com/2018/09/20/why-amsterdam-is-jealous-of-americas-growing-weed-industry.html

[25] *Leary v. United States*, 395 U.S. 6 (1969); Yasmin Tayag, *Timothy Leary's Arrest For Marijuana Possession Still Matters 50 Years Later*, INVERSE (Mar. 13, 2016), https://www.inverse.com/article/12782-timothy-leary-s-arrest-for-marijuana-possession-still-matters-50-years-la

[26] Graza, F. (2016, March 23). Nixon advisor: We created the war on drugs to "criminalize" black people and the anti-war left. Retrieved from Quartz: https://qz.com/645990/nixon-advisor-we-created-the-war-on-drugs-to-criminalize-black-people-and-t

[27] Armentano, P. (n.d.). 35 Years of Prohibition. Retrieved from

NORML: https://norml.org/component/zoo/category/
celebrating-35-years-of-failed-pot-policies

[28] Stroup, K. (2017, September 28). On the Passing of Hugh
Hefner. Retrieved from NORML: https://blog.norml.org/2017/09/
28/on-the-passing-of-hugh-hefner/

[29] Associated Press. (1977, March 15). Carter Asks Congress to
Decriminalize Marijuana Possession. Retrieved from The New York
Times: https://www.nytimes.com/1977/03/15/archives/
carter-asks-congress-to-decriminalize-marijuana-possession-cocaine.html

[30] Dufton, E. (2019, April 25). Why the 1970s Effort to
Decriminalize Marijuana Failed. Retrieved from Smithsonian
Magazine: https://www.smithsonianmag.com/history/
why-1970s-effort-decriminalize-marijuana-failed-180972038/

[31] A Brief History of the Drug War. (n.d.). Retrieved from Drug
Policy   Alliance: https://www.drugpolicy.org/issues/
brief-history-drug-war

[32] Goldberg, S. B. (1993, May 25). NOT-SO-SECRET
INGREDIENT. Retrieved from The Chicago Tribune:
https://www.chicagotribune.com/news/
ct-xpm-1993-05-25-9305250146-story.html

[33] Bonni, J. (2003, February 11). US MA: Column: You Down
With MPP? Retrieved from Media Awareness Project:
http://www.mapinc.org/drugnews/v03/n237/a06.html?127

[34] (A Brief History of the Drug War, n.d.)

[35] (Colorado Marijuana Legalization Initiative, Amendment 64
(2012), n.d.)

[36] Bartels, L. (2012, September 21). Tom Tancredo backs
marijuana measure. Retrieved from The Denver Post:
http://blogs.denverpost.com/thespot/2012/09/21/
tom-tancredo-backs-marijuana-ballot-measure/82193/

[37] Pasquariello, A. (2017, November 7). GOP backer of 2012 Colorado marijuana legalization vote: "Experiment in liberty is working". Retrieved from The Cannabist: https://www.thecannabist.co/2017/11/07/tom-tancredo-colorado-marijuana-legalization-2012-vote-anniversary/91893/

[38] Breathes, W. (2012, Novemeber 1). The history of cannabis in Colorado...or how the state went to pot. Retrieved from Westword: https://www.westword.com/news/the-history-of-cannabis-in-coloradoor-how-the-state-went-to-pot-5118475

[39] Ferner, M. (2012, November 6). Amendment 64 Passes: Colorado Legalizes Marijuana For Recreational Use. Retrieved from Huff Post: https://www.huffpost.com/entry/amendment-64-passes-in-co_n_2079899?guccounter=2

[40] NAACP Endorses WA's Marijuana Initiative. (2012, August 27). Retrieved from Snohomish Times: http://www.snohomishtimes.com/snohomishNEWS.cfm?inc=story&newsID=2503

[41] Connelly, J. (2011, September 18). State Dems: Legalize marijuana. Retrieved from Seattle PI: https://blog.seattlepi.com/seattlepolitics/2011/09/18/state-dems-legalize-marijuana/

[42]McKinley, J. (2012, March 7). Pat Robertson Says Marijuana Use Should be Legal. Retrieved from The New York Times: https://www.nytimes.com/2012/03/08/us/pat-robertson-backs-legalizing-marijuana.html?_r=2

[43] (The History of Cannabis Museum, n.d.)

[44] NPR/PBS NewsHour/Marist Poll . (2019, Juli). Retrieved from Marist: http://maristpoll.marist.edu/wp-content/uploads/2019/07/NPR_PBS-NewsHour_Marist-Poll_USA-NOS-and-Tables_1907190926.pd

[45] Bennett, P. (2016, July 28). What are trichomes and why do they exist on cannabis? Retrieved from Leafly: https://www.leafly.com/news/cannabis-101/what-are-trichomes-on-cannabis

[46] Ibid.

[47] Phytocannabinoid. (n.d.). Retrieved from Weed Maps: https://weedmaps.com/learn/dictionary/phytocannabinoid/

[48] Full Spectrum vs Broad Spectrum vs CBD Isolate: Difference Explained. (2020). Retrieved from RoyalCBD.com: https://royalcbd.com/cbd-isolate-vs-full-spectrum-broad-spectrum/

[49] Smith, N. (2019, September 26). Cannabis research pioneer hopes latest discovery is not overlooked — again. Retrieved from NBC News: https://www.nbcnews.com/tech/innovation/cannabis-research-pioneer-hopes-latest-discovery-not-overlooked-again-n

[50] Full Spectrum vs Broad Spectrum vs CBD Isolate: Difference Explained. (2020). Retrieved from RoyalCBD.com: https://royalcbd.com/cbd-isolate-vs-full-spectrum-broad-spectrum/

[51] Earlenbaugh, E. (2015, March 12). What Is CBN (Cannabinol) & What Are the Benefits of This Cannabinoid? Retrieved from Leafly: https://www.leafly.com/news/science-tech/what-is-cbn-and-what-are-the-benefits-of-this-cannabinoid

[52] Beadle, A. (2020, February 7). CBG vs CBD: What Are the Differences? Retrieved from Analytical Cannabis: https://www.analyticalcannabis.com/articles/cbg-vs-cbd-what-are-the-differences-312232

[53] Rehm, D. W. (2015, January 30). Comparative risk assessment of alcohol, tobacco, cannabis and other illicit drugs using the margin of exposure approach. Retrieved from NCBI: https://www.ncbi.nlm.nih.gov/pmc/articles/PMC4311234/

[54] Does marijuana negatively impact mental health? (n.d.).

Retrieved from Drug Policy Alliance: https://www.drugpolicy.org/does-marijuana-negatively-impact-mental-health

[55] Marijuana Break Staff. (2020, March 3). The Best Cannabis Strains For Mood Swings. Retrieved from Marijuana Break: https://www.marijuanabreak.com/cannabis/ailments/best-marijuana-strains-for-controlling-mood-swings

[56] Franciosi, A. (2016). The 7 Stages Of Being High. Retrieved from Honest Marijuana: https://honestmarijuana.com/being-high/#more-643

[57]List of names for cannabis. (2020, April 17). Retrieved from Wikipedia: https://en.wikipedia.org/wiki/List_of_names_for_cannabis

[58] Leafly Staff. (2020, February 5). The best strains of all time: 100 popular cannabis strains to try before you die. Retrieved from Leafly: https://www.leafly.com/news/strains-products/top-100-marijuana-strains

[59] Quirk, M. B. (2017, September 27). Sorry, Colorado — New Law Means No More Weed Gummy Bears. Retrieved from Consumer Reports: https://www.consumerreports.org/consumerist/sorry-colorado-new-law-means-no-more-weed-gummy-bears/

[60] Angell, T. (2019, September 5). Hemp Farming Quadrupled In The U.S. This Year, New Report Shows. Retrieved from Forbes: https://www.forbes.com/sites/tomangell/2019/09/05/hemp-farming-quadrupled-in-the-u-s-this-year-new-report-shows/#3fde763

[61] 5 ANCIENT USES OF HEMP. (2019, May 5). Retrieved from Purekana: https://purekana.com/blogs/news/5-ancient-uses-of-hemp/

[62] General Hemp Information. (2020). Retrieved from Hemp Basics: https://www.hempbasics.com/shop/general-hemp-information

[63] Biehl, Z. (2019, May 3). The Amazing World of Hemp: Hempcrete - the Most Sustainable Building Material on Earth. Retrieved from Cannabis Tech: https://www.cannabistech.com/articles/hemp-hempcrete-the-most-sustainable-building-material-on-Earth/

[64] Steinbuch, Y. (2016, May 6). This car is made out of cannabis hemp. Retrieved from The New York Post: https://nypost.com/2016/05/06/this-car-is-made-out-of-cannabis-hemp/

[65] Stanley. (2020). Cannabis Reports. Retrieved from Hemp Uses: Top Uses for Hemp: https://cannabisreports.org/hemp-uses-top-uses-for-hemp/

[66] Everything Hemp USA (2019, March 23). 5 Other Uses for Hemp You May Not Know About: https://www.greenentrepreneur.com/article/331065

[67] NHA News. (2019, November 25). Hemp: Our Solution to The Climate Change? Retrieved from National Hemp Association: https://nationalhempassociation.org/hemp-our-solution-to-the-climate-change/

[68] Basics. (2020). Retrieved from Hemp Tech Global: https://hemptechglobal.com/styled-17/page83/page83.html

[69] Brown, B. (2019). Cannabis: The Illegalization of Weed in America. New York: First Second.

[70] How many birds die from plastic pollution? (2018, October 9). Retrieved from WWF: https://www.wwf.org.au/news/blogs/how-many-birds-die-from-plastic-pollution#gs.26vp3f

[71] Adams, M. (2019, August 22). These Congressional Republicans Support the Cannabis Industry. Retrieved from The Fresh Toast: https://thefreshtoast.com/cannabis/these-congressional-republicans-support-the-cannabis-industry/

[72] Drug Scheduling. (n.d.). Retrieved from DEA:

https://www.dea.gov/drug-scheduling

[73] Shortt, D. (2019, May 30). USDA Says States Should Not Interfere With Hemp Transportation. Retrieved from Harris Bricken: https://harrisbricken.com/cannalawblog/ usda-says-states-should-not-interfere-with-hemp-transportation/

[74] KTVB Staff. (2019, September 26). Truck drivers sentenced for transporting hemp through Idaho. Retrieved from KTVB: https://www.ktvb.com/article/news/crime/ truck-drivers-sentenced-for-transporting-hemp-through-ada-county-idaho/ 277-48d9ec07-b224-4623-b556-2291f5bcdf3b

[75]States With Marijuana Decriminalization. (2020). Retrieved from   NORML: https://norml.org/aboutmarijuana/item/ states-that-have-decriminalized

[76]Misulonas, J. (2020). 15 Largest Cities That Have Decriminalized   Marijuana.   Retrieved   from   Civilized: https://www.civilized.life/articles/ largest-cities-decriminalized-marijuana/

[77]Local Decriminalization. (2020). Retrieved from NORML: https://norml.org/legal/local-decriminalization

[78] Misulonas, J. (2020). 15 Largest Cities That Have Decriminalized   Marijuana.   Retrieved   from   Civilized: https://www.civilized.life/articles/ largest-cities-decriminalized-marijuana/

[79] Examining Marijuana Arrests. (2012, April 2). Retrieved from The New York Times: https://www.nytimes.com/2012/04/02/ opinion/examining-marijuana-arrests.html

[80] Voytko, L. (2019, July 29). New York Decriminalizes Recreational Marijuana, Falls Short Of Governor's Goal To Legalize. Retrieved from Forbes: https://www.forbes.com/sites/lisettevoytko/ 2019/07/29/

new-york-decriminalizes-recreational-marijuana-falls-short-of-governors

[81]Nunley, K. (2018, December 12). NEW YORK GOVERNOR TO UNVEIL PLAN TO LEGALIZE MARIJUANA IN 2019. Retrieved from Medical Marijuana Inc.: https://www.medicalmarijuanainc.com/news/new-york-governor-legalize-marijuana-2019/

[82] Jaeger, K. (2020, March 8). Virginia Lawmakers Send Marijuana Decriminalization Bill To Governor's Desk. Retrieved from Marijuana Moment: https://www.marijuanamoment.net/virginia-lawmakers-send-marijuana-decriminalization-bill-to-governors-(

[83] FERNANDEZ, J.-G. (2020, March 17). Virginia Drastically Liberalizes Marijuana Laws. Retrieved from Shepherd Express: https://shepherdexpress.com/hemp/cannabis/virginia-drastically-liberalizes-marijuana-laws/

[84] Virginia Medical Cannabis FAQs. (2018). Retrieved from Virginia NORML: https://www.vanorml.org/faqs

[85] Moomaw, G. (2019, October 17). A Democratic takeover could make Virginia more marijuana-friendly. But legalization may still be years away. Retrieved from Virginia Mercury: https://www.virginiamercury.com/2019/10/17/a-democratic-takeover-could-make-virginia-more-marijuana-friendly-but

[86] Leafly Staff. (2020, January 29). Qualifying conditions for medical marijuana by state. Retrieved from Leafly: https://www.leafly.com/news/health/qualifying-conditions-for-medical-marijuana-by-state

[87]Leonard, N. (2018, April 8). Medical Marijuana Patients Struggle with Costs. Retrieved from Press of Atlantic City: https://www.pressofatlanticcity.com/wellness/medical-marijuana-patients-struggle-with-costs/article_2b4d51f3-d792-5625-87f9-5870eafdbae2.html

[88]Esposito, L. (2020, February 26). CBD Oil for Treating Epilepsy. Retrieved from U.S. News & World Report: https://health.usnews.com/conditions/brain-disease/epilepsy/articles/cbd-oil-for-treating-epilepsy

[89] Bienenstock, D. (2020, June 25). Dr. Lester Grinspoon encouraged America to 'reconsider' marijuana. Retrieved from Leafly: https://www.leafly.com/news/politics/dr-lester-grinspoon-encouraged-america-to-reconsider-marijuana

[90] Medical Marijuana Patient Numbers. (2020, May 9). Retrieved from Marijuana Policy Project: https://www.mpp.org/issues/medical-marijuana/state-by-state-medical-marijuana-laws/medical-marijuana-patient-numbers/

[91] O'Malley, N. (2020, January 10). Medical Cannabis Industry Continues Robust Oklahoma Growth. Retrieved from Sooner Politics: https://www.soonerpolitics.org/nigel-omally/medical-cannabis-industry-continues-robust-oklahoma-growth

[92] Lockhart, B. (2018, April 10). LDS Church issues statement on proposed Utah marijuana initiative. Retrieved from Desert News: https://www.deseret.com/2018/4/10/20643178/lds-church-issues-statement-on-proposed-utah-marijuana-initiative

[93] Cohen, R. (2017, March 27). Would legalizing medical marijuana help curb the opioid epidemic? Retrieved from Reuters: https://www.reuters.com/article/us-health-addiction-medical-marijuana-idUSKBN16Y2HV

[94] Rogers, B. (2018, December 4). Utah has a new medical marijuana law — but not the one approved by voters in the recent election. Retrieved from The Salt Lake Tribune: https://www.sltrib.com/news/politics/2018/12/03/utah-house-passes-medical/

[95] McGreevy, P. (2019, August 30). California lawmakers OK

medical marijuana in K-12 schools. Will Newsom approve? Retrieved from The LA Times: https://www.latimes.com/california/story/2019-08-30/medical-marijuana-california-schools-legislation-newsom

[96] Nelson, B. (2020, March 10). You can't be fired in N.J. for failing drug test because of medical marijuana, court rules. Retrieved from NJ.com: https://www.nj.com/marijuana/2020/03/nj-medical-marijuana-patients-win-big-protections-from-being-fired-for-f

[97] Keshner, A. (2019, November 12). Amazon wrongly fired a worker and 'blacklisted' him for using medical marijuana, lawsuit alleges. Retrieved from Market Watch: https://www.marketwatch.com/story/amazon-wrongly-fired-a-worker-and-blacklisted-him-for-using-medical-m

[98] Costa, C. D. (2015, June 5). How Employee Drug Testing Targets the Poor and Minorities. Retrieved from Cheatsheet.com: https://www.cheatsheet.com/money-career/how-employee-drug-testing-targets-the-poor-and-minorities.html/

[99] Angell, T. (2020, March 6). Joe Biden Is Frustrated People Think He Still Believes Marijuana Is A Gateway Drug. Retrieved from Forbes: https://www.forbes.com/sites/tomangell/2020/03/06/joe-biden-is-frustrated-people-think-he-still-believes-marijuana-is-a-gatew

[100] Saulsberry, G. (2020, February 21). Compassionate Care Foundation opens Atlantic City dispensary, The Botanist. Retrieved from NJBiz.com: https://njbiz.com/welcome-ad/?retUrl=/compassionate-care-foundation-opens-atlantic-city

[101] Yang, L. (2017, April 19). The Real Difference Between Body Highs and Head Highs. Retrieved from Vice: https://www.vice.com/en_us/article/7xzb7z/science-of-head-and-body-highs-weedweek2017

[102] Rutherford, A. (2018, July 12). These States Have The Best Chance Of Legalizing Marijuana. Retrieved from Pot Network:

https://www.potnetwork.com/news/
these-states-have-best-chance-legalizing-marijuana

[103] Crowe, M. (2018, July 26). Recreational marijuana: How Michigan's potential legalization compares to other states. Retrieved from Click on Detroit: https://www.clickondetroit.com/all-about-michigan/2018/07/26/recreational-marijuana-how-michigans-potential-legalization-compares-to-o•

[104] Cammenga, J. (2019, April 24). How High Are Taxes on Recreational Marijuana in Your State? Retrieved from Tax Foundation: https://taxfoundation.org/2019-recreational-marijuana-taxes/

[105] Folley, A. (2019, May 25). Colorado governor signs law legalizing marijuana social use areas. Retrieved from The Hill: https://thehill.com/homenews/state-watch/446078-colorado-governor-signs-law-legalizing-marijuana-social-use-areas

[106] Tom Schuba, R. H. (2020, January 1). Thousands flock to weed shops as Illinois' pot prohibition comes to an end. Retrieved from Chicago Sun Times: https://chicago.suntimes.com/cannabis/2020/1/1/21045915/legal-marijuana-recreational-pot-illinois-dispensaries-first-day-open

[107] (Jaeger, Illinois Governor Pardons Over 11,000 People For Marijuana One Day Before Legal Sales Begin, 2019)

[108] Ulloa, D. (2019, October 25). Cannabis Reform and Politics at NJ Democratic Conference. Retrieved from Heady NJ: https://headynj.com/cannabis-reform-politics-at-nj-dems-conference/

[109] Johnson, B. (2019, November 18). Legalizing weed will be decided by N.J. voters in referendum next year, top lawmaker says. Retrieved from NJ.com: https://www.nj.com/marijuana/2019/11/voters-will-decide-next-year-if-new-jersey-should-legalize-weed-top-lawmake•

[110] Why We Must End Cannabis Prohibition In New Jersey.

(2019, November 6). Retrieved from YouTube: https://www.youtube.com/ watch?v=wQilF2QvjIk&feature=youtu.be&fbclid=IwAR2hmskbIGdRxı

[111]Moran, T. (2019, November 24). This I Have Never Seen: Sue Altman, Anti-Norcross Activist Yanked from Senate Hearing by State Police. Retrieved from NJ.com: https://www.nj.com/opinion/ 2019/11/ this-i-have-never-seen-sue-altman-an-anti-norcross-activist-yanked-from-s

[112]Wood, S. (2019, December 16). N.J. voters to decide on legalizing marijuana. Retrieved from Philly Inquirer: https://www.inquirer.com/business/weed/ cannabis-marijuana-new-jersey-senate-vote-ballot-amendment-to-legalize-

[113] (Jaeger, Marijuana Companies Urged Governor To Ban Cannabis Home Cultivation, Document Shows, 2019)

[114] Pace, D. (1999, October 22). Pot Users Invade Barr Office. Retrieved from Cannabis News.com: http://cannabisnews.com/news/ 3/thread3387.shtml

[115] Incredibly Unique Art. (2020). Retrieved from Fine Art America: https://fineartamerica.com/featured/ 10-john-brown-american-abolitionist-photo-researchers.html?product=cɛ

[116] Oleinic, A. (2019, June 20). BDS Analytics, Arcview Project $40B In Global Cannabis Spending By 2024. Retrieved from Benzinga: https://www.benzinga.com/markets/cannabis/19/06/ 13946649/ bds-analytics-arcview-project-40b-in-global-cannabis-spending-by-2024

[117] About. (2020). Retrieved from Oaksterdam University: https://oaksterdamuniversity.com/about/

[118] An online medical cannabis program. (2020, May 3). Retrieved from Campus News: https://cccnews.info/2020/05/03/ an-online-medical-cannabis-program/

[119] Minor in Cannabis Studies. (n.d.). Retrieved from Stockton University: https://stockton.edu/general-studies/cannabis-studies.html

[120] How to Get Hired to Work in the Legal Cannabis Industry Part 3: Getting Hired as a Grower. (2015, March 12). Retrieved from Leafly: https://www.leafly.com/news/industry/how-to-get-hired-to-work-in-the-medical-cannabis-industry-part-3

[121] Yakowicz, W. (n.d.). How CPAs, Tax Lawyers are Fighting the IRS for Marijuana. Retrieved from Inc.com: https://www.inc.com/will-yakowicz/how-cpas-tax-lawyers-fighting-irs-for-marijuana.htmlh

[122] Using medical cannabis to address addiction disorders. (2019, November 14). Retrieved from Medical Cannabis Network: https://www.healtheuropa.eu/using-medical-cannabis-to-address-addiction-disorders/94903/

[123] Our Mission. (2019). Retrieved from Mary and Main: https://maryandmain.com/about/

[124]CannaTech Team. (2016, June 16). WEED – A CNN Special Report by Dr. Sanjay Gupta. Retrieved from Canna Tech: https://www.canna-tech.co/uncategorized/weed-a-cnn-special-report-by-dr-sanjay-gupta/

[125]Schroyer, J. (2020, April 2). US markets that have allowed marijuana businesses to remain open during coronavirus pandemic stay-at-home orders. Retrieved from MJ Biz Daily: https://mjbizdaily.com/states-that-have-allowed-marijuana-businesses-to-remain-open-during-corona

[126] Smith, N. (2019, September 26). Cannabis research pioneer hopes latest discovery is not overlooked — again. Retrieved from NBC News: https://www.nbcnews.com/tech/innovation/cannabis-research-pioneer-hopes-latest-discovery-not-overlooked-again-n1059

[127] Breathes, W. (2012, Novemeber 1). The history of cannabis in Colorado...or how the state went to pot. Retrieved from Westword: https://www.westword.com/news/ the-history-of-cannabis-in-coloradoor-how-the-state-went-to-pot-51184

[128] The Associated Press. (2018, January 4). What is the Cole memo and what does it have to do with legal pot? Retrieved from Kiro 7: https://www.kiro7.com/news/local/ what-is-the-cole-memo-and-what-does-it-have-to-do-with-legal-pot/ 676279936/

[129] Jarrett, L. (2018, January 4). Sessions nixes Obama-era rules leaving states alone that legalize pot. Retrieved from CNN: https://www.cnn.com/2018/01/04/politics/jeff-sessions-cole-memo/ index.html

[130] Holden, D. (2019, January 15). Bill Barr Says He's "Not Going After" Marijuana In States Where It's Legal. Retrieved from Buzzfeed News: https://www.buzzfeednews.com/article/ dominicholden/ bill-barr-attoreny-general-marijuana-legal-enforcement

[131] Jaeger, K. (2020, June 23). Attorney General Wasted DOJ Resources To Investigate Marijuana Mergers Due To Personal Bias, Official Alleges. Retrieved from Marijuana Moment: https://www.marijuanamoment.net/ attorney-general-wasted-doj-resources-to-investigate-marijuana-mergers-

[132] Koop, E. (2020, March 4). States turn to unenforced federal law to slow medical marijuana legalization. Retrieved from Roll Call: https://www.rollcall.com/2020/03/04/ states-turn-to-unenforced-federal-law-to-slow-medical-marijuana-legaliz

[133] Jaeger, K. (2019, June 19). Congress Clashes On Marijuana Amendments In Floor Debate. Retrieved from Marijuana Moment: https://www.marijuanamoment.net/

congress-clashes-on-marijuana-amendments-in-floor-debate/

[134]Nunley, K. (2018, June 11). TRUMP SIGNALS HE'S WILLING TO BACK FEDERAL MARIJUANA BILL. Retrieved from Medical Marijuana Inc.: https://www.medicalmarijuanainc.com/news/trump-federal-marijuana-bill/

[135] Poll suggests Californians want more adult-use marijuana stores. (2019, October 1). Retrieved from MJ Biz Daily: https://mjbizdaily.com/poll-suggests-californians-want-more-adult-use-marijuana-stores/

[136] Forecasts Hazy for State Marijuana Revenue. (2019, August 19). Retrieved from Pew Trusts: https://www.pewtrusts.org/en/research-and-analysis/issue-briefs/2019/08/forecasts-hazy-for-state-marijuana-revenue

[137] (Smith, Pew report: Recreational cannabis tax revenues remain volatile, 2019)

[138] CARLESSO, K. M. (2019, August 19). New report shows recreational marijuana revenue volatile in many states. Retrieved from The CT Mirror: https://ctmirror.org/2019/08/19/new-report-shows-recreational-marijuana-revenue-volatile-in-many-states/

[139] Prat Vallabhaneni, J. K. (2019, October 11). White & Case Discusses Cannabis Banking Bill's Implications for Financial Services. Retrieved from COLUMBIA LAW SCHOOL'S BLOG ON CORPORATIONS AND THE CAPITAL MARKETS: https://clsbluesky.law.columbia.edu/2019/10/11/white-case-discusses-cannabis-banking-bills-implications-for-financial-service

[140] H.R.1595 - Secure And Fair Enforcement Banking Act of 2019. (2019, September 25). Retrieved from Congress.gov: https://www.congress.gov/bill/116th-congress/house-bill/1595/cosponsors?q=%7b%22search%22:%5b%22SAFE+Banking+Act%22%5d%

[141] Jaeger, K. (2019, May 21). All 50 State Banking Associations

Urge Congress To Pass Marijuana Financial Services Bill. Retrieved from Marijuana Moment: https://www.marijuanamoment.net/all-50-state-banking-associations-urge-congress-to-pass-marijuana-financi

[142] Marijuana Banking Update. (2019, March 31). Retrieved from Fincen.gov: https://www.fincen.gov/sites/default/files/shared/285053%202Q%20FY2019%20Marijuana%20Banking%20Update_Pub

[143] (Reinicke, 2019)

[144] McBride, S. (2019, August 30). The Reason Pot Stocks Will Never Recover. Retrieved from Forbes: https://www.forbes.com/sites/stephenmcbride1/2019/08/30/the-reason-pot-stocks-will-never-recover/#4e0f9a557030

[145] (RTTNews, 2019)

[146] Kumar, K. (2019, June 25). Oregon Marijuana Market Has Too Much Weed, Price Is Dropping. Retrieved from International Business Times: https://www.ibtimes.com/oregon-marijuana-market-has-too-much-weed-price-dropping-2802849

[147] Benchaabane, N. (2020, January 20). Fumbled numbers? Rejected pot applicants in Missouri point to scoring flaws. Retrieved from St. Louis Post-Dispatch: https://www.stltoday.com/news/local/marijuana/fumbled-numbers-rejected-pot-applicants-in-missouri-point-to-scoring/article_e974e7c4-8654-5f15-a66e-e594262c5b32.html

[148] Graham, D. A. (2015, November 3). Why Did Ohio's Marijuana-Legalization Push Fail? Retrieved from The Atlantic: https://www.theatlantic.com/politics/archive/2015/11/where-did-ohios-marijuana-legalizers-go-wrong/414061/

[149] 'South Park' Parodies MedMen's 'The New Normal' Ad. (2019, July 26). Retrieved from Now This News: https://nowthisnews.com/videos/weed/south-park-parodies-medmens-the-new-normal-ad

[150] Swenson, A. (2020, April 16). Arizona's Marijuana Activists Are United. Will That Be Enough for Legalization This Year? Retrieved from Phoenix New Times: https://www.phoenixnewtimes.com/news/ arizonas-marijuana-activists-are-united-behind-the-smart-and-safe-act-is-that

[151] (Smith, 2019)

[152] Inspection Detail. (2020, February 12). Retrieved from OSHA: https://www.osha.gov/pls/imis/ establishment.inspection_detail?id=1417453.015

[153] Sacirbey, O. (2017, June 15). Analysts: High Times sale could buoy cannabis industry. Retrieved from MJ Biz Daily: https://mjbizdaily.com/ analysts-high-times-purchase-buoy-cannabis-industry/

[154] Ibid.

[155] Alpert, B. (2018, December 4). Marijuana Stock Aphria Is Falling Again as It Fights a Short Seller Who Called Out 'Something Very Sinister'. Retrieved from Barrons: https://www.barrons.com/ articles/ marijuana-stock-aphria-down-on-short-seller-report-1543855963

[156] (Securities and Exchange Commission v. John M. Fife and Clarion Management, LLC., 2007)

[157] The Motley Fool. (2019, June 7). After plagued by a scandal, where are shares of Aphria (APHA) headed? Retrieved from Stock News: https://stocknews.com/news/ apha-after-plagued-by-a-scandal-where-are-shares-of-aphria/

[158] AMENDMENT NO. 2 REGISTRATION STATEMENT UNDER THE SECURITIES ACT OF 1933. (2018, May 23). Retrieved from UNITED STATES SECURITIES AND EXCHANGE COMMISSION: https://www.sec.gov/Archives/ edgar/data/1589149/000172186818000457/f2msrt052118s1a.htm

[159] Schlesinger, J. (2019, June 17). Florida businessman agrees to proposed judgment in $27 million 'lucrative market manipulation,' SEC filing says. Retrieved from CNBC: https://www.cnbc.com/2019/06/17/sec-proposed-judgment-with-primary-strategist-in-27-million-lucrative-ma

[160] Ibid.

[161] Alpert, B. (2018, December 4). Marijuana Stock Aphria Is Falling Again as It Fights a Short Seller Who Called Out 'Something Very Sinister'. Retrieved from Barrons: https://www.barrons.com/articles/marijuana-stock-aphria-down-on-short-seller-report-1543855963

[162] Winds Research. (2019, June 12). MassRoots: A Sustainable Business Model Remains Elusive. Retrieved from Seeking Alpha: https://seekingalpha.com/article/4269822-massroots-sustainable-business-model-remains-elusive

[163] Dickson, E. (2019, August 28). Counterfeit Weed Vape Cartridges Are Everywhere — and They're Making People Sick. Retrieved from The Rolling Stone: https://www.rollingstone.com/culture/culture-features/counterfeit-thc-vapes-cdc-vaping-health-alert-875931/

[164] Branfalt, T. (2020, February 5). California Will Require Cannabis QR Codes. Retrieved from Ganjapreneur: https://www.ganjapreneur.com/california-to-require-cannabis-qr-codes/

[165] COMMERCIAL CANNABIS QUICK RESPONSE CODE CERTIFICATE. (2020, February 12). Retrieved from BUREAU OF CANNABIS CONTROL : https://bcc.ca.gov/law_regs/20200212_addendum_foe.pdf

[166] Hughes, T. (2020, March 8). 'Scary for everybody': This is what it's like in Seattle and King County, areas under siege from the

coronavirus. Retrieved from USA Today: https://www.usatoday.com/story/news/health/2020/03/08/coronavirus-seattle-king-county-practicing-social-distancing/4971187002/

[167] CANNABUSINESS. (n.d.). Retrieved from SXSW: https://www.sxsw.com/conference/cannabusiness/

[168] Charlotte's Web CNN Special Dr Sanjay Gupta. (2015, January 5). Retrieved from YouTube: https://www.youtube.com/watch?v=PKvbaIiLKvE

[169] Proper Staff. (2019, January 15). Why Is Everyone Obsessed With California's Emerald Triangle? Retrieved from A Proper High: https://aproperhigh.com/articles/why-is-everyone-obsessed-with-california-s-emerald-triangle

[170] ACLU. (2020, April 20). A Tale of Two Countries: Racially Targeted Arrests in the Era of Marijuana Reform. Retrieved from ACLU: https://www.aclu.org/sites/default/files/field_document/042020-marijuanareport.pdf

[171] Seal Misdemeanor Marijuana Conviction Records. (2017). Retrieved from Colorado General Assembly: https://leg.colorado.gov/bills/hb17-1266

[172] Norcia, A. (2018, September 25). Jersey's Weedman Is the Hero America Needs. Retrieved from Vice: https://www.vice.com/en_us/article/zm5enw/jerseys-weedman-is-the-hero-america-needs

[173] I Sold Weed in Front of My Governor's Office. (n.d.). Retrieved from Vice: https://video.vice.com/en_us/video/i-sold-weed-in-front-of-my-governors-office/5bad6ae5be407769e12b024a

[174] Lawson, K. (2019, May 13). Illegal Marijuana Grows In Pacific Northwest Declined After Legalization, Study Finds. Retrieved from Marijuana Moment: https://www.marijuanamoment.net/

illegal-marijuana-grows-in-pacific-northwest-declined-after-legalization-《

[175] Marijuana Justice Coalition Asserts Statement of Principles on Federal Marijuana Reform. (2019, July 9). Retrieved from Human Rights Watch: https://www.hrw.org/news/2019/07/09/marijuana-justice-coalition-asserts-statement-principles-federal-marijuan

[176] ACLU. (2020, April 20). A Tale of Two Countries: Racially Targeted Arrests in the Era of Marijuana Reform. Retrieved from ACLU: https://www.aclu.org/sites/default/files/field_document/042020-marijuanareport.pdf

[177] Ibid.

[178] Evans, M. D. (2015). The Consequences of Conviction. Retrieved from Colorado State Public Defenders.

[179] (Drug Scheduling, n.d.)

[180] Fertig, P. D. (2019, September 9). Why the most pro-marijuana Congress ever won't deal with weed. Retrieved from Politico: https://www.politico.com/story/2019/09/09/marijuana-congress-1712973

[181] Marijuana conviction in Pennsylvania? Apply for pardon now, Lt. Gov. John Fetterman says. (2019, September 26). Retrieved from WTAE: https://www.wtae.com/article/marijuana-conviction-pardons-pennsylvania-john-fetterman/29248145

[182] Cheung, K. (2019, September 26). Applying for a marijuana pardon in Pennsylvania. Retrieved from Local 21 News: https://local21news.com/news/local/applying-for-a-marijuana-pardon-in-pennsylvania

[183] Martino, P. (2019, September 25). Pa. Governor Tom Wolf Supports Legalizing Marijuana. Retrieved from Pittsburgh CBS Local: https://pittsburgh.cbslocal.com/2019/09/25/tom-wolf-marijuana-legalization/

[184] Hill, E., Tiefenthäler, A., Triebert, C., Jordan, D., Willis, H., & Stein, R. (2020, June 8). 8 Minutes and 46 Seconds: How George Floyd Was Killed in Police Custody. Retrieved from New York Times: https://www.nytimes.com/2020/05/31/us/ george-floyd-investigation.html

[185] Atmonavage, J. (2020, April 23). NJ.com. Retrieved from He was a big-time pot trafficker, now aging in a N.J. prison. Should he get released amid the coronavirus outbreak?: https://www.nj.com/ coronavirus/2020/04/ he-was-a-big-time-pot-trafficker-now-aging-in-a-nj-prison-should-he-get-rele

[186] Livio, S. K. (2017, November 11). With Phil Murphy's win, it's 'full steam ahead' for legal marijuana. Retrieved from NJ.com: https://www.nj.com/politics/2017/11/ hold_murphys_victory_is_the_first_step_toward_a_ma.html

[187] Nichols, J. (2018, August 30). Cynthia Nixon's Emphasis on Marijuana Legalization Added Vital Thinking to the New York Gubernatorial Debate. Retrieved from The Nation: https://www.thenation.com/article/archive/ cynthia-nixons-emphasis-on-marijuana-legalization-added-vital-thinking-to-t

[188] Sloat, S. (2018, April 3). The 2018 Midterms: Five Politicians Who Want to Legalize and Tax Marijuana. Retrieved from Inverse: https://www.inverse.com/article/ 43172-2018-midterms-pro-marijuana-candidates

[189] Smiley, D. (2018, November 7). How Andrew Gillum lost Florida's governor's race. Retrieved from Tampa Bay: https://www.tampabay.com/florida-politics/buzz/2018/11/07/ why-andrew-gillum-lost-floridas-governor-race/

[190] Cohen, R. M. (2018, November 7). WHY BEN JEALOUS LOST THE MARYLAND GOVERNOR'S RACE. Retrieved from The Intercept: https://theintercept.com/2018/11/07/

maryland-governor-election-ben-jealous-larry-hogan/

[191] Jaeger, K. (2020, February 25). Presidential Candidates Clash Over Marijuana Legalization At Democratic Debate. Retrieved from Marijuana Moment: https://www.marijuanamoment.net/presidential-candidates-clash-over-marijuana-legalization-at-democratic-c

[192] Jaeger, K. (2019, September 17). Bernie Sanders Asks Campaign Rally Audience To Share Stories About Marijuana Arrests. Retrieved from Marijuana Moment: https://www.marijuanamoment.net/bernie-sanders-asks-campaign-rally-audience-to-share-stories-about-marij

[193] Sanez, A. (2019, May 16). Joe Biden supports decriminalizing marijuana, stops short of calling for legalization. Retrieved from CNN: https://www.cnn.com/2019/05/16/politics/joe-biden-marijuana-decriminalization/index.html

[194] LIFT EVERY VOICE: THE BIDEN PLAN FOR BLACK AMERICA. (2020). Retrieved from Biden for President: https://joebiden.com/blackamerica/

[195] Gomez, H. (2019, October 2). Marriage Equality Is Joe Biden's Legacy. He Had To Evolve To Get There. Retrieved from Buzzfeed News: https://www.buzzfeednews.com/article/henrygomez/joe-biden-gay-marriage-equality

[196] Hutzler, A. (2018, August 24). Legal Weed: How Republicans Learned to Love Marijuana. Retrieved from Newsweek: https://www.newsweek.com/2018/08/24/legal-weed-republicans-love-marijuana-1072761.html

[197] Ingold, J. (2014, January 1). World's First Legal Recreational Marijuana Salles Begin in Colorado. Retrieved from The Denver Post: https://www.denverpost.com/2014/01/01/worlds-first-legal-recreational-marijuana-sales-begin-in-colorado/

[198] (2020, April 22). Retrieved from Senator Jacky Rosen:

https://www.rosen.senate.gov/sites/default/files/2020-04/
042220%20-%20Rosen-Wyden%20Letter%20on%20COVID-19%20Supp

[199] Lopez, G. (2020, January 23). Marijuana legalization is about to have a huge year. Retrieved from Vox: https://www.vox.com/policy-and-politics/2020/1/23/21076978/marijuana-legalization-2020-ballot-initiatives

[200] Schreiner, B. (2020, March 4). Foes push back against medical marijuana bill in Kentucky. Retrieved from Seattle Times: https://www.seattletimes.com/seattle-news/health/foes-push-back-against-medical-marijuana-bill-in-kentucky/

[201] House passes medical cannabis bill in 65-30 vote; pandemic derails progress in Senate. (2020, April 7). Retrieved from Marijuana Policy Project: https://www.mpp.org/states/kentucky/

[202] Edward, T. (2020, March 12). Tennessee Senate Passes Medical Marijuana Legalization Bill—But There's A Catch. Retrieved from High Times: https://hightimes.com/news/tennessee-senate-passes-medical-marijuana-legalization-bill-but-theres-a-catc

[203] Tennessee marijuana laws lag behind other states. (2020, April 20). Retrieved from Marijuana Policy Project: https://www.mpp.org/states/tennessee/

[204] Lee, Y. (2019, October 25). Arizona: Competing Initiatives Raise Questions About 2020 Legalization. Retrieved from Cannabiswire: https://cannabiswire.com/2019/10/25/arizona-competing-initiatives-raise-questions-about-2020-legalization/

[205] Swenson, A. (2020, January 2). MedMen, a Top Donor for Arizona Pot Legalization, Abandons Its Arizona Licenses. Retrieved from Phoenix New Times: https://www.phoenixnewtimes.com/marijuana/marijuana-cannabis-medmen-arizona-selling-investments-financial-1141907

[206] 2020 Marijuana Policy Reform Ballot Campaigns. (2020,

April   23).   Retrieved   from   Marijuana   Policy   Project: https://www.mpp.org/policy/ballot-initiatives/

[207] Jaeger, K. (2020, February 26). Vermont House Approves Bill to Legalize Marijuana Sales. Retrieved from Marijuana Moment: https://www.marijuanamoment.net/ vermont-house-approves-bill-to-legalize-marijuana-sales/

[208]Marcelo, P. (2020, March 9). Boston's First Recreational Marijuana   Shop   Opens.   Retrieved   from   WGBH: https://www.wgbh.org/news/local-news/2020/03/09/ boston-braces-for-large-crowds-as-1st-pot-shop-opens

Don't miss out!

Visit the website below and you can sign up to receive emails whenever Daniel Ulloa publishes a new book. There's no charge and no obligation.

https://books2read.com/r/B-A-DIMK-MEDFB

BOOKS 2 READ

Connecting independent readers to independent writers.

Lightning Source UK Ltd.
Milton Keynes UK
UKHW020938141122
412173UK00011B/2409